THE KIDS' EASY AIR FRYER COOKBOOK

SALLY MORGAN

SCHOLASTIC

Published in the UK by Scholastic, 2024
1 London Bridge, London, SE1 9BG
Scholastic Ireland, 89E Lagan Road, Dublin Industrial Estate, Glasnevin, Dublin, D11 HP5F

SCHOLASTIC and associated logos are trademarks and/or
registered trademarks of Scholastic Inc.

Text © Sally Morgan, 2024
Illustrations by Jamie Gregory © Scholastic, 2024
Photographs © Adobe Stock, Getty Images and Shutterstock, 2024
Photograph on page 82 © Rachel Crew

ISBN 9780 7023 3934 9

A CIP catalogue record for this book is available from the British Library.

The recipes in this cookbook contain lots of different ingredients. Some ingredients will not
be suitable for everyone, please review all ingredients before cooking to make sure they are
suitable for you, your family and your friends and carefully check all food labels.

Scholastic do not have control over the ingredients you use to make these recipes or the
environment in which you are making them in. Be aware of cross contamination and always
thoroughly clean your preparation area before and after use. Be cautious of hot surfaces and
sharp edges when cooking to make sure you, your family and your friends stay safe.

Printed in China

Paper made from wood grown in sustainable forests and other controlled sources.

3 5 7 9 10 8 6 4 2

www.scholastic.co.uk

KEY TO THE SYMBOLS IN THIS BOOK:

(VG) = Vegetarian   (VE) = Vegan   (GF) = Gluten Free

CONTENTS

INTRODUCTION

Have you ever looked at a food and thought, "Can I air fry that?" Maybe not, but get ready, because once you discover just how many tasty treats you can create with just the turn of a dial and the push of a button, you soon will. Inside this book you will find more than 50 delicious and ridiculously easy-to-follow recipes as well as tips to help you to chef up, or create, many more of your very own.

Read on to discover all you need to know to begin your delicious journey to air-fryer-chef super stardom! What are you waiting for?

HOW DO AIR FRYERS WORK?

An air fryer cooks food by circulating hot air around it with a fan. The hot air crisps and browns the food without having to dunk it in hot oil. Air fryer baskets and trays contain holes that allow the air to move around the food quickly, cooking it from all sides.

What type of fryer do you have?

AIR FRYER OVEN
Does your air fryer have a door that you can open with removable racks and trays inside? This is an air fryer oven. Air fryer ovens tend to be larger than cylindrical basket-type air fryers and may have more functions such as toast, dehydrate, roast and steam. For the recipes in this book you will only need to use the air-fry function of your oven. The trays and or baskets inside your air fryer oven get very hot. Make sure to always use oven gloves or tongs when attempting to remove them from your fryer.

BASKET AIR FRYERS
Does your air fryer have a drawer with a handle that you can use to remove it from the fryer? This is a basket air fryer. Basket air fryers tend to be smaller than air fryer ovens, but that means they take up less space on your worktop. The handle of the air fryer basket makes it easy to remove so that you can turn the food without having to touch hot surfaces.

All the recipes contained in this book have been tested in both an air fryer oven and a basket air fryer, which means you will be able to make the recipes no matter which type you have; however, it is very important to read the handbook that came with your air fryer.

Every model of air fryer is a bit different. The instructions in the handbook will give you specific information on how to use your air fryer safely. It will also give you useful tips on how get the best results from your fryer, such as how long it takes the air fryer to preheat and how to clean it so it's ready to go next time.

WHY AIR FRY?

IT'S EASY
Set the time and the temperature and let the air fryer do the rest.

IT'S SPEEDY
Air fryers cook food quickly by blasting it with hot air propelled by powerful fans.

IT'S HEALTHY
Air fryers use a lot less oil than conventional oil frying so you can recreate some of your favourite fried foods with a lot less fat.

IT'S ECO-FRIENDLY
Air fryers use less electricity than conventional ovens because they are smaller and cook more quickly.

IT'S LESS MESSY
Air fryers and their accessories are easy to clean compared to bulk oven trays or greasy oil fryer baskets. Just soak the basket or rack in hot water with dishwashing liquid while you enjoy your food!

IT'S SAFE
Provided that you follow the safety instructions that come with your air fryer, air frying is much safer than conventional oil frying.

A GUIDE TO SAFE AIR FRYING

BEFORE FRYING

- Always check with a responsible adult before using your air fryer.
- Make sure your air fryer is clean and sitting on a stable flat surface.
- Read the recipe through first to make sure you have everything you need.
- Gather and prepare the ingredients and equipment you are going to need.
- Ask for help if you need it!

WHILE FRYING

- Make sure to always use oven mitts and tongs when touching hot surfaces and food inside your fryer.
- Don't be a stranger! Check in on your food while it is cooking.
- Never put air fryer liner papers inside the basket of your fryer during the preheating stage or without food on top of them.

AFTER FRYING

- Be really careful when removing hot food or baking dishes from the air fryer. Always use oven gloves or tongs, and ask an adult to help if you need it.
- Do not eat food straight out of the fryer. IT'S HOT! Leave it to cool for 5–10 minutes.
- Make sure that food cooked inside the air fryer is piping hot right through.

TIPS FOR SUCCESSFUL AIR FRYING

WATCH THE TIME
The recipes in this book suggest how long your food will take to cook, but all air fryers are different. Some air fryers cook quickly whereas others might take a bit longer. To ensure you get the best results from your air fryer, make sure to check on your food while it is cooking.

GIVE IT SOME SPACE
Take care not to overfill your fryer. Air fryers cook food by surrounding it with hot air. Crowding the basket of your air fryer stops the air from moving around the food and prevents it from cooking evenly.

MANAGE YOUR EXPECTATIONS
Air fryers are great, but they don't get the same results as regular frying. Foods cooked in the air fryer may not get quite as crisp and golden as fried foods, but they are just as delicious.

AIR FRYING EQUIPMENT

Air fryers don't need lots of fancy accessories to make delicious food, but here is a list of a few useful tools that make air frying easier, safer and much more fun!

OIL SPRAY

Air fryers can cook your food without oil, but spraying some foods with a little spritz of oil before air frying helps them to become crisp and golden.

THERMOMETER

If you don't already have one, a digital meat or probe thermometer is a useful, potentially lifesaving tool in the kitchen.

Raw foods such as meat and poultry can contain harmful bacteria that can make you very unwell. Cooking food to a high temperature kills bacteria and makes the food safe to eat. When air frying, it is important to make sure that your food is cooked all the way through and that the heat from the air fryer has made it to the middle of the piece of food. Using a meat thermometer is a quick and easy way to be sure that your food is piping hot all the way through and safe to eat.

These thermometers can be found in kitchen shops or online.

SILICONE CUPCAKE CASES

Silicone is good for air frying because it can withstand high temperatures and is easy to clean. Reusable silicone cupcake cases come in lots of bright colours and are perfect for making small batches of cakes and muffins. Unlike paper, silicone cupcake cases are strong enough to use without a baking tin.

EGG MOULDS

Unlike ring egg moulds you may use with a frying pan, air fryer egg moulds have a bottom to stop the egg from leaking through holes in the air fryer basket. Air fryer egg moulds are made from silicone, or metal with a non-stick coating.

RAMEKINS

The recipes in this book have been created for ramekins that are 9 cm diameter and 5 cm deep, or roughly 200 ml capacity. If you have different sized ramekins, you will need to adjust the cooking temperature and time.

TONGS

Everyone knows that if you touch things that are very hot, you will get burned. Stop this from happening by making sure you do not touch the inside of your fryer or anything that has just come out of the fryer using your bare hands. Always use tongs to put food into the hot air fryer, to turn it or move it inside the basket and to remove it from the fryer.

OVEN GLOVES

Tongs are great for picking up small pieces of food, but bigger things, such as egg moulds or ramekins, can be more difficult. A good pair of oven gloves, or a single glove, alongside tongs in your other hand should make it easy to get food out of the fryer.

AIR FRYER LINER PAPER

Air fryer liner papers stop foods from sticking to the inside of your fryer. Air fryer liners are precut to the size of your air fryer basket. They are non-stick and may also have small holes cut in to allow air to circulate throughout the fryer and crisp the food. Some liners don't have holes in them, but these are fine to use too, you just might need to turn the food over during the cooking process.

Only use air fryer lining papers with food on top of them. Never use liner papers when preheating your air fryer as they can fly around the basket and catch fire.

HEATPROOF MAT

Never put anything that has just come out of your air fryer onto your worktop. Always put it onto a plate or a heatproof mat. Heatproof mats are made from plastic, fabric or wood and will protect your worktop from burning or melting.

That's about it. All that's left now is to choose what you want to make first. Prawn fajitas? Halloumi fries? Marshmallow sliders? Check with an adult, gather all of the ingredients and gear you need, and get cooking!

BREAKFAST

AMERICAN PANCAKES

MAKES 6 PANCAKES | TAKES 25 MINUTES

Unlike the pancakes you might have on Pancake Day, American breakfast pancakes are thick and fluffy and are eaten all year round. Serve your pancakes with fresh fruit and a drizzle of honey or maple syrup.

INGREDIENTS:

120 g plain flour

1 tsp baking powder

½ tsp bicarbonate of soda

240 ml buttermilk

1 egg, beaten

14 g butter, melted

60 g chocolate chips

Butter or oil spray

EQUIPMENT:

6 egg moulds or 8–10 silicone cupcake cases

1. Add the flour, baking powder and bicarbonate of soda to a large bowl and stir.

2. Pour the buttermilk, egg and melted butter into the flour mixture and stir well. Keep mixing until you have a thick batter with no lumps. Add the chocolate chips and stir.

3. Grease the egg moulds by dipping a piece of kitchen roll in butter and rubbing the butter around the insides. Alternatively, spray the insides of your moulds with oil.

4. If your moulds are bottomless, put an air fryer liner into the basket of your air fryer, and then place the moulds inside. If your moulds have a bottom, place them directly into the air fryer basket. There is no need to preheat for this recipe.

5. Spoon batter into the moulds until it reaches approximately 1.5 cm up the side of the mould. The mixture is pretty thick so you may need to spread it out with the back of a spoon.

6. Set the temperature to 180°C/350°F and the timer to 5 minutes.

7. When the time is up, carefully use tongs to turn your pancakes out of the moulds onto the basket of your fryer. The air fryer will be hot, so ask an adult for help here if you need it. The pancakes should slip out of the moulds easily. Cook for a further 3 minutes.

8. When your pancakes are done, carefully use tongs to remove them from the fryer. The air fryer will be hot, so ask an adult for help here if you need it. Serve with maple syrup or honey.

Don't have egg moulds? Use silicone cupcake cases to make pancake bites instead. If using silicone cupcake cases, reduce the cooking time to 4 minutes and then insert a cocktail stick into the pancake bite. If the stick is clean when you pull it out, the bites are done!

If the stick has raw batter on it when you pull it out, put the bites back in the fryer for 1–2 more minutes and then check again.

CHEF IT UP!

Feeling fruity? Swap the chocolate chips for 60 g of blueberries. Yum!

CINNAMON FRENCH TOAST STICKS

SERVES 4 | TAKES 15-20 MINUTES

Impress your family with these sweet, easy-to-make breakfast treats. Delicious dusted with icing sugar or drizzled with golden syrup. Serve with your favourite fresh fruit.

INGREDIENTS:

4 thick slices of bread

2 large eggs

4 tbsp milk

1 tbsp sugar

1 tsp cinnamon

A pinch of salt

Oil spray

Icing sugar or golden syrup to serve

1 Cut each slice of bread into thick strips, around 2–3 cm wide.

2 Crack the eggs into a bowl. Add the milk, sugar, cinnamon and salt to the bowl. Beat the ingredients together using a fork.

3 Dip the bread sticks into the egg mix one at a time. Turn each stick over to make sure each side is coated with the mix.

4 Preheat the air fryer to 200°C/400°F. When the air fryer has preheated, spray the basket with oil.

5 Carefully use tongs to put the sticks into the fryer basket, about 2 cm apart. The air fryer will be hot, so ask an adult for help here if you need it. Do not crowd the basket or the sticks will not cook evenly. If they don't all fit, put the rest to one side to cook when the first batch is done.

6 Set the timer for 4 minutes. When the time is up, open the fryer and carefully turn the sticks over using tongs. The air fryer will be hot, so ask an adult for help here if you need it. Cook for another 3 minutes.

7 When the time is up, carefully remove the sticks from the fryer using tongs.

8 Serve immediately, dusted with icing sugar or drizzled with golden syrup.

CHEESY EGG BITES

MAKES 4-6 EGG BITES | TAKES 25 MINUTES

These cheesy bites are delicious and packed with protein that will keep you full until lunchtime.

INGREDIENTS:

3 large eggs

½ small red pepper, chopped

¼ small onion, chopped

30 g cheese, grated

1 tbsp milk

Salt

Pepper

Chopped parsley for garnish

EQUIPMENT:

4–6 silicone cupcake cases

1. Crack the eggs into a jug and beat with a fork. Add the milk and beat again.

2. Add the chopped pepper, onions and grated cheese. Add a pinch of salt and freshly ground black pepper and stir until everything is combined.

3. Pour the egg mix into the silicone cupcake cases. This mixture should make enough to fill at least four cases to three quarters full.

4. Preheat the fryer to 180°C/350°F. When it has preheated, use tongs to carefully put the egg bites into the basket and set the timer to 10 minutes. The air fryer will be hot, so ask an adult for help here if you need it.

5. When the time is up, check on your egg bites. They should be firm and not wobbly. If they are wobbly, or you can see any raw egg, cook them for 2–3 more minutes and then check again.

6. Carefully use tongs to remove your egg bites from the fryer basket and place them on a plate to cool for 2–3 minutes. The air fryer will be hot, so ask an adult for help here if you need it.

7. Turn your bites out of the silicone cases and serve, garnished with chopped parsley.

BACON AND EGG BREAKFAST SANDWICH

SERVES 1 | TAKES 20 MINUTES

Lots of fast-food restaurants are known for their breakfast sandwiches, but none will taste quite as good as this one, fresh from your very own air fryer.

INGREDIENTS:

1 bagel, sliced

2 bacon slices

1 egg

1 slice of cheese (optional)

EQUIPMENT:

1 egg mould or ramekin

1. Preheat the air fryer to 200°C/400°F.

2. When the fryer is hot, use tongs to carefully place the two slices of bacon into the basket, towards the back. Set the timer to 7 minutes. You can use an air fryer liner here if you like.

3. Spray the egg mould or ramekin with a little oil. Crack the egg into the mould.

4. When the time is up, open the fryer and use tongs to carefully put the egg mould into the basket, in front of the bacon. The air fryer will be hot, so ask an adult for help here if you need it. Set the timer to 6 minutes.

5. When the time is up, open the fryer. If the bacon looks crispy, carefully remove it from the fryer using tongs. If the white of your egg looks solid, with no runny, clear bits, carefully remove the ramekin using tongs and place onto a heatproof mat. The air fryer will be hot, so ask an adult for help here if you need it. If either the bacon does not look as crispy as you would like, or the egg still seems a little runny, close the fryer and cook for another 2–3 minutes before checking again. Place the bacon onto a piece of kitchen roll.

6. Place the two pieces of bagel into the air fryer open side up. Set the timer to 2 minutes.

7. When the time is up, carefully remove the bagel from the fryer using tongs. Place the bottom half onto a plate and put the slice of cheese on top. Next add the bacon and the egg.

8. Top with a little salt and pepper before putting on the top of the bagel. Serve immediately with ketchup or brown sauce.

CHEF IT UP!

Try cooking a sausage alongside as shown in the picture.

If cooking a sausage with the bacon, put the sausage in first for 5 minutes, before adding the bacon, as sausages take a little longer to cook. If the sausage is thick, split it in half lengthwise to help it to cook quicker. Check the sausage is cooked by pushing a meat thermometer into it. If the temperature reads 75°C/165°F, it's ready to serve. Mushrooms work great in the air fryer too!

CHOCOLATE CHUNK GRANOLA

MAKES 4-6 SERVINGS | TAKES 2 HOURS

This granola recipe is packed full of fibre and protein. Enjoy on it own, with milk or on top of your favourite yoghurt.

INGREDIENTS:

5 tbsp honey

½ tsp salt

2 tbsp vegetable oil

250 g rolled oats

50 g pumpkin seeds

50 g sunflower seeds

50 g sliced almonds

50 g chopped walnuts

50 g chocolate chips (dark, milk or white is fine, whatever your preference!)

1. Preheat the air fryer to 140°C/280°F.

2. Add the honey, salt and oil to a large bowl. Use a fork or a whisk to mix them together. Add the oats, pumpkin and sunflower seeds, almonds and walnuts and stir until all the dry ingredients are coated in oil and honey.

3. Carefully place a liner into the basket of your air fryer. Spread a 2–3 cm layer of the granola mixture on top of the liner. The air fryer will be hot, so ask an adult for help here if you need it. You may need to work in batches. Set the timer to 30 minutes.

4. When the time is up, open the fryer. The granola should look crisp and golden. If it looks a little pale, return the basket to the fryer and cook for another 4–5 minutes.

5. When the granola is done, remove the basket from the fryer and sprinkle the top of the granola with chocolate chips. Leave the granola to cool in the fryer basket for 10–15 minutes.

6. When the time is up, use the back of the spoon to spread the now-melted chocolate across the top of the granola.

7. Use a spatula to slide the liner with the granola out of the fryer basket onto a plate. Put the plate in the fridge to chill for 30 minutes.

8. When the granola is cool and the chocolate is set, break up the granola into bite-size chunks. This granola can be stored in an airtight container in the fridge for up to a week.

Warning! This recipe contains nuts. Make sure none of your family or friends have nut allergies before sharing this granola with them.

CHEF IT UP!

Try adding any nuts and dried fruit that you like. Dark chocolate chips work wonderfully with dried cherries!

EGG IN A BASKET

SERVES 1 | TAKES 15 MINUTES

Make this quick and easy egg-in-toast recipe the next time you want a hot breakfast in a hurry.

INGREDIENTS:

1 thick slice of bread

1 medium egg

1. Preheat the air fryer to 200°C/400°F.

2. Put the slice of bread onto a cutting board. Place the bottom of a drinking glass into the middle of the slice of bread and press it down to make a dent. Remove the glass and press around the circle with your fingers.

3. Carefully place a liner into the basket of the air fryer and use tongs to put the slice of bread in, dent side up.

4. Crack the egg into a small bowl. Carefully tip the egg into the dent in the bread. Sprinkle on a pinch of salt and pepper.

5. Close the fryer and set the timer to 6 minutes.

6. When the time is up, open the fryer. The bread should look toasted and the egg should be firm on top. If the egg looks a little raw, or wobbly, cook for another 2 minutes before checking again.

7. Carefully remove the slice from the fryer using tongs or a spatula. The air fryer will be hot, so ask an adult for help here if you need it. Serve immediately, garnished with any herbs or spices that you like.

HONEY NUT BREAKFAST BARS

MAKES 6-8 SLICES | TAKES 35-45 MINUTES

Packed with fruit and nuts, these bars are a filling breakfast that is quick to grab when you need to get out of the door fast.

INGREDIENTS:

150 g honey

125 g butter

250 g rolled oats

½ tsp salt

80 g flaked almonds

½ apple, grated

100 g raisins

50 g dried apricots, chopped

EQUIPMENT:

Cake tin that fits in your air fryer

Baking paper

1 Place the butter in a microwave-safe jug or bowl and add the honey. Microwave on high for 20 seconds, then stir. If the butter is fully melted, move on to the next step, if not, put the butter back in the microwave and heat for another 20 seconds. Repeat until the butter is fully melted. Stir well to combine the honey with the melted butter. Put to one side.

2 Add the oats to a large bowl, then add the salt. Tip in the almonds, grated apple and dried fruit and stir. Add the honey-butter mixture and mix well. Preheat the air fryer to 160°C/320°F.

3 Place your cake tin on a piece of baking paper and draw around it with a pencil. Cut out the piece of paper. Dip a piece of kitchen roll in butter and rub it around the inside of the tin. Put the piece of paper into the bottom of the tin, on top of the butter.

4 Spoon the mixture into the prepared tin. Press the mixture into the corners and smooth it out with the back of the spoon. Carefully put the tin into the basket of the air fryer. Set the timer to 25 minutes.

5 When the time is up, open the fryer. The oat-bar mix should look golden brown. If it isn't, put it back into the air fryer for 5–10 minutes and check again. When it looks golden brown, put on oven gloves and carefully remove the tin from the fryer. The air fryer will be hot, so ask an adult for help here if you need it. Leave it to cool for 30 minutes.

6 When the tin is cool, run a table knife around the inside of the tin to free the oat-bar mix from the sides.

7 Cut into 6–8 equally sized breakfast bars while still in the tin, and remove using a table knife or metal spatula. Store in an airtight container. These will stay fresh for up to a week.

Warning! This recipe contains nuts. Make sure none of your family or friends have nut allergies before sharing these bars with them.

CHEF IT UP!

Swap out the almonds for any nut you like. Shelled sunflower seeds, chia or flaxseeds work well too!

CINNAMON SWIRLS

MAKES 10 CINNAMON SWIRLS | TAKES 45 MINUTES

Flaky, buttery pastry with a sweet, cinnamon filling, these breakfast treats will fill your kitchen with an aroma you will want to wake up to every day.

INGREDIENTS:

2 tbsp soft brown sugar

1 tbsp ground cinnamon

¼ tsp ground nutmeg (optional)

1 x 320 g pack ready-rolled puff pastry

1 tbsp plain flour

For the glaze (optional):

60 g icing sugar

1–2 tbsp water

1 Add the sugar, cinnamon and nutmeg, if you're using it, to a small bowl. Mix the ingredients together using a fork.

2 Sprinkle the flour onto a clean worktop. Unroll the sheet of pastry onto the floured surface.

3 Sprinkle the cinnamon sugar onto the sheet of pastry. Take care to cover the whole sheet in an even layer.

4 Starting at one of the short sides, roll up the pastry like a Swiss roll. Wrap the roll in cling film and put in the fridge to chill for 30 minutes.

5 Remove the wrapped roll from the fridge and preheat the air fryer to 200°C/400°F.

6 Unwrap the roll and put it on a cutting board. Carefully use a sharp knife to cut the roll into 2.5 cm thick slices.

7 Carefully place a paper liner into the basket of the air fryer. Carefully place the slices into the basket using tongs. The air fryer will be hot, so ask an adult for help here if you need it. Try to leave at least 3 cm around each slice. You may need to work in batches. Set the timer to 10 minutes.

8 When the time is up, open the fryer. The swirls should have spread out and look crisp and golden brown. If they look a little pale, cook for another 2–3 minutes before checking again.

9 Carefully remove the swirls from the fryer using tongs and leave them to cool on a wire rack. The air fryer will be hot, so ask an adult for help here if you need it.

10 If you would like to add a drizzle of icing, put the icing sugar in a bowl and slowly add the water, bit by bit, until you have reached the desired consistency. Use a spoon to drizzle the icing over the pastries.

PEACH DANISH

MAKES 6 PASTRIES | TAKES 25 MINUTES

Traditional Danish pastries are made with a flaky dough that contains yeast which can be tricky to make. This recipe uses ready-made puff pastry to create fabulously fruity breakfast pastries in a matter of minutes.

INGREDIENTS:

1 x 320 g pack ready-rolled puff pastry

6–12 tbsp tinned custard

12 peach slices (roughly half a tin)

1 egg, beaten

1 tbsp flour

EQUIPMENT:

Pastry brush

Rolling pin

1. Sprinkle flour onto a clean worktop. Unroll the sheet of puff pastry onto the flour and smooth it out.

2. Use a table knife to cut the rectangle in half lengthways. This will make two long strips. Use the same knife to cut each strip into three squares measuring approximately 10 x 10 cm. This will make 6 squares.

3. Put one of the squares of pastry onto the floured worktop diagonally, so that one corner is close to you.

4. Spoon 1–2 tablespoons of custard into the centre of the square. Take two slices of peach and place them on the custard in a line from the top corner of the pastry to the bottom.

5. Fold the left corner into the centre over the peaches and then fold the right corner over the left as if you were tucking the peaches up in bed. Fasten the pastry together with a little beaten egg.

6. Slide a spatula under your pastry and place it on a liner paper.

7. Repeat steps 3 to 6 to make another pastry and place it on your liner paper at least 3 cm from the first. Arrange as many pastries as you can on your liner paper.

8. Preheat the air fryer to 180°C/350°F.

9. When the fryer is hot, open it up and carefully lower your liner paper into the basket. Ask an adult for help here if you need it. Set the timer to 14 minutes.

10. When the time is up, open your fryer and check your pastries. They should have puffed up and look crisp and golden. If they still look a little pale, put them back in the fryer for 2 minutes and then check again.

11. When they are ready, carefully remove your pastries from the fryer using tongs and leave them to cool on a wire rack.

Out of peaches? No problem! Try using any fruit you have – blueberries, strawberries, tinned pears or even a few teaspoons of jam will be just as delicious.

CHEF IT UP!

To make your pastries look extra fancy, dust with icing sugar before serving.

SCONES

MAKES ABOUT 6 SMALL SCONES | TAKES 30 MINUTES

These scones are delicious served with butter, jam and even a blob of clotted cream. Yum!

INGREDIENTS:

175 g self-raising flour

½ tsp baking powder

A pinch of salt

30 g butter, cold

1 tbsp sugar

2 tbsp milk

1 egg, beaten

EQUIPMENT:

Grater

Rolling pin

5 cm cutter

1. Put the flour, sugar, baking powder and salt into a medium sized bowl and mix well.

2. Grate the cold butter into the flour. Rub the butter into the flour using your fingertips until the mixture looks like coarse sand.

3. Add the egg and 1 tablespoon of the milk and bring the mixture together using your hands. If the mixture looks a little dry, add the second tablespoon of milk and continue using your hands until you have a soft dough.

4. Sprinkle a little flour onto a clean worktop. Take the dough out of the bowl and place it onto the flour.

5. Preheat the air fryer to 180°C/350°F.

6. Use a rolling pin to roll out your dough until it is 3 cm thick. Use your cutter to press out as many circles as you can from the dough. Gather up the rest of the dough and roll it out to cut out some more. Brush the tops of your scones with a little milk using a pastry brush.

7. Carefully put the scones into the basket of your air fryer. Try to leave a few centimetres around each one in case they spread. You may need to work in batches. Set the timer to 8 minutes.

8. When the time is up, open the fryer. If the scones look risen and golden, carefully remove them from the fryer using tongs. If they look a little pale, close the fryer and cook for 2–3 more minutes before checking again.

9. Leave them to cool on a wire rack. Serve with jam and clotted cream.

CHEF IT UP!

Try adding some raisins or dried cranberries. For a spicier scone, crystallized ginger works well too!

LUNCH

CHEESE AND ONION PASTY

MAKES 4 PASTIES | TAKES 30 MINUTES

Make your own cheese and onion pasties, just like the ones that come from your favourite high-street bakery. These pasties are delicious hot or cold, which makes them perfect for packed lunches or picnics!

INGREDIENTS:

120 g potato, peeled and cut into ½ cm cubes

100 g onion, chopped

120 g cheddar cheese, grated

½ tsp mustard powder

1 egg, beaten

½ tsp salt

½ tsp black pepper

1 x 320 g pack ready-rolled puff pastry

CHEF IT UP!

Substitute the cheddar for feta, or your favourite blue cheese!

1   Mix the potato, onion, cheese and mustard powder in a medium bowl using a wooden spoon. Add about half of the beaten egg and the salt and pepper before stirring again.

2   Cut the sheet of pastry into four equal rectangles using a table knife. Preheat the air fryer to 190°C/375°F.

3   Spoon a quarter of the cheese mixture onto the bottom half of one of the rectangles. Leave a 2 cm gap between the mixture and the bottom edge and sides of the pastry.

4   Use a pastry brush to brush a little water around the edges of the pastry. This will help to seal the pastry and to keep the filling inside while it is cooking. If you don't have a pastry brush, use your fingers to dab some water around the edge, just make sure that you've dried your hands before moving onto step 5.

5   Fold the top half of the pastry over the filling. If you find that you do not have enough pastry to cover the filling, scoop some of it out, using a teaspoon. Seal the pastry closed by pressing the edges together using your fingertips. Repeat steps 3–5 with the remaining rectangles of pastry.

6   Brush the remaining egg over the tops of your pastries. Poke the top of each pastry with a fork. This will make small holes that allow steam to escape from inside of the pastry as it cooks, and will help to stop them from bursting open.

7   Carefully place a lining paper into the basket of the air fryer and arrange the pastries onto the liner, using tongs or a spatula. Leave at least 5 cm around each pastry. You may need to work in batches. Store the remaining pastries in the fridge until you are ready to air fry them. Set the timer to 15 minutes.

8   When the time is up, open the fryer. The pastries should have puffed up and look crisp and golden brown. If they look paler than you would like, close the fryer and cook for another 3 minutes before checking again.

9   When the pastries are crisp and golden, carefully turn them over using tongs. Set the timer to 3 minutes. This will make sure the bottom of the pastry is crisp and not soggy. Carefully remove the pastries from the fryer using tongs and leave them to cool for 10 minutes before serving.

CHICKEN SPRING ROLLS

SERVES 2-4 | TAKES 1 HOUR 15 MINUTES

Spring rolls originated in China but are now enjoyed all over the world.

INGREDIENTS:

1 tbsp soy sauce

1 tsp cornflour

1 tbsp rice wine vinegar

250 g minced chicken

2 tbsp vegetable oil

2 cloves garlic, finely grated

3 cm piece of ginger, finely grated

2 spring onions, chopped

150 g cabbage, shredded

2 carrots, coarsely grated

2 tbsp oyster sauce

1 tsp sesame oil

8–10 x 20 cm x 20 cm square spring roll wrappers

1 Mix the soy sauce, cornflour and rice wine vinegar in a medium sized bowl. Add the chicken and mix. Let the chicken sit in the sauce for 10–15 minutes.

2 Heat a large frying pan over a medium-high heat and add 1 tablespoon of vegetable oil. Carefully add the chicken to the pan. Break up any large clumps of chicken using a wooden spoon. Stir the chicken as it cooks.

3 Cook the chicken for 8–10 minutes or until it has all turned brown and is starting to look crisp and golden in places. Turn off the heat and empty the pan into a clean bowl, scraping out any stuck-on bits using a spatula.

4 Return the pan to the hob and heat 1 tablespoon of vegetable oil over a medium-high heat. Add the garlic, ginger and spring onion and cook for 1 minute while stirring with a wooden spoon to stop it from sticking to the bottom of the pan. It doesn't matter if it sticks a little bit, but if it looks like it is starting to burn, turn down the heat and skip to the next step.

5 Add the cabbage and grated carrots and cook for another 5 minutes while continuing to stir.

6 When the cabbage is starting to soften, add the oyster sauce and sesame oil and return the cooked chicken to the pan. Stir the ingredients together and heat for a further 2–3 minutes.

7 Turn off the heat and empty the contents of the pan onto a large plate and set aside until cool.

8 Place a spring roll wrapper on a flat plate or chopping board so that one of the corners is pointing towards you. Cover the remaining wrappers with a piece of damp kitchen roll.

9 Put 2 tablespoons of the cooled filling onto the wrapper about 2 cm in from the corner closest to you.

10 Fold the corner closest to you over the filling and start to roll towards the opposite corner. Just before you get halfway up the wrapper, fold the two side corners inwards over the filled part of the roll.

11 Continue to roll towards the top corner. Dampen the top corner with a little water and roll the filled part of the spring roll over the top. Put your finished roll to one side, with the seam underneath.

12 Repeat steps 8–11 with the rest of your filling. This recipe should make enough to fill 8–10 spring rolls.

13 Preheat the air fryer to 200°C/400°F. Once the air fryer has preheated, use tongs to carefully arrange the spring rolls in the basket, seam-side down, 2–3 cm apart. The air fryer will be hot, so ask an adult for help here if you need it. Spray or brush your spring rolls with a little oil. This will help them to turn golden.

14 Set the timer to 8 minutes. When the time is up, open your air fryer and carefully turn over your spring rolls using tongs. Set the timer to 5 minutes.

15 When the time is up, open your fryer. If the rolls look golden and crisp, carefully remove them from the fryer using tongs. If they look a little pale, cook for another 2–3 minutes.

16 Leave to cool for at least 5 minutes before serving. They will be hot! Serve with sweet chilli, soy sauce or any of your favourite dipping sauces.

Can't find spring roll wraps? Use filo pastry instead. Cut the filo into 20 cm x 20 cm squares and lay one sheet on top of another before filling.

CHEF IT UP!

Experiment with different fillings such as pork, tofu, beansprouts or cooked rice noodles.

VEGETABLE SAMOSAS

SERVES 4-6, MAKES 20 SAMOSAS | TAKES 45-60 MINUTES

Samosas are a popular street food that originated in the Middle East and South Asia but are now enjoyed all over the world. These crispy vegetable samosas make a delicious lunch and are easy to make.

INGREDIENTS:

1 medium potato, diced

2 tbsp vegetable oil

1 medium onion, chopped

1 tsp mustard seeds

2 cm piece of ginger, grated

100 g frozen peas

1 tbsp ground coriander

1 tsp ground cumin

1 tsp mild chilli powder

1 tsp curry powder

½ tsp salt

½ pack filo pastry

Oil spray

1 Put the diced potato into a microwave-safe bowl and add 3 tablespoons of water. Cover the bowl with a plate and microwave on high for 5 minutes. When the time is up, carefully remove the bowl from the microwave using oven gloves. Drain the potatoes using a colander and put to one side.

2 Heat the oil in a frying pan over a medium heat. When the oil is hot, carefully add the onion, mustard seeds and ginger. Stir and cook until the onions are soft, which should take about 3–5 minutes.

3 Add the frozen peas and give the pan a good stir. Add the coriander, cumin, chilli powder, curry powder and salt to the pan and stir well before adding the potatoes. Turn the heat down to low and cook for a further ten minutes, stirring occasionally to make sure the mixture is not sticking to the bottom of the pan. Leave to cool.

4 Unroll the sheets of filo pastry and cut in half lengthways using kitchen scissors. Peel off two strips and lay them on top of one another, with the short end closest to you. Cover the rest with a clean, damp tea towel to stop them drying out.

5 Dollop 1 tablespoon of your cooled mixture onto the nearest end of the strip. Take the right-hand corner of the pastry and fold it over the mixture to make a triangle shape at the end of the pastry. Take the left-hand corner and fold it straight up the strip. The mixture is now enclosed on two sides. Take the left corner and fold it towards the right-hand edge of the strip, then fold the triangle straight up. The mixture should now be enclosed on all three sides. Keep folding the pastry in the same way until you are at the end of the strip. Tuck any remaining pastry under the parcel.

6 Place the samosas into the basket of your air fryer at least 3 cm apart and spray, or brush, with a little oil. They won't all fit at once, so you will need to work in batches. There is no need to preheat for this recipe.

7 Set the air fryer to 200°C/400°F and the timer for 5 minutes. When the time is up, open the fryer. The samosas should look crisp and golden. If the samosas are looking a little pale, cook them for a further 2 minutes.

8 When they are golden, open the fryer and use tongs to carefully turn the samosas over. Brush or spray the samosas with a little oil and then cook for another 2 minutes.

9 When the time is up, carefully remove the samosas from the fryer using tongs. The air fryer will be hot, so ask an adult for help here if you need it.

10 Let them cool for at least 5 minutes before serving.

CHEF IT UP!
These are perfect served with a mango chutney or minty yoghurt raita.

(VG)

CHEESY BEAN QUESADILLA

SERVES 1 | TAKES 10 MINUTES

There are few greater partnerships in the world than grated cheese and baked beans. In this, their latest adventure, the dynamic duo meet inside a flour tortilla. This recipe, while not even slightly authentically Mexican, makes a delicious lunch or snack for one.

INGREDIENTS:

1 large flour tortilla

3 tbsp baked beans

30 g cheddar cheese, grated

A pinch of salt

A grind of black pepper

1 Preheat the air fryer to 180°C/350°F.

2 Spoon the baked beans onto one half of the tortilla. Squash the baked beans with a fork to mash them into the sauce. Season with a little salt and pepper.

3 Sprinkle the grated cheese over the beans.

4 Fold the bare half of the tortilla over to cover the cheese and beans.

5 Carefully put the filled tortilla into the basket of the air fryer. It's a good idea to ask an adult for help here if you need to. Set the timer to 5 minutes.

6 When the time is up, open the fryer and turn the quesadilla over using tongs. The air fryer will be hot, so ask an adult for help here if you need it. Set the timer to 3 minutes.

7 When the time is up, carefully remove the quesadilla from the fryer using tongs. Again, as the air fryer is hot, ask an adult for help here if you need it. Leave to cool for 2 minutes before cutting into triangles using kitchen scissors. Serve warm.

CHEF IT UP!

Don't stop at cheese and beans! Cheese and onion? Tuna and sweetcorn? Chocolate chips and marshmallows?!

NAAN PIZZAS

MAKES 4 | TAKES 15 MINUTES

These naan pizzas are a great lunch and are quick and easy to make.

INGREDIENTS:

4 mini naans

8 tbsp pizza sauce or tomato passata

1 tsp garlic powder

1 tsp dried basil

1 tsp dried oregano

12 slices pepperoni

150 g mozzarella, grated

CHEF IT UP!

Experiment with your favourite toppings – olives, tuna, peppers and artichokes are all great choices!

1. Mix the pizza sauce or tomato passata, garlic powder, dried basil and oregano together in a small bowl.

2. Spread the seasoned sauce onto one side of each naan using a spoon.

3. Top each naan with three slices of pepperoni and sprinkle each of them with a quarter of the grated cheese.

4. Place the naans into the basket of your air fryer. There is no need to preheat for this recipe. You may need to do them in batches.

5. Set the fryer to 160°C/320°F and the timer to 10 minutes.

6. When the time is up, open the fryer and look at your pizzas. The cheese should have melted and be brown in places. If the pizzas don't look quite ready, close the fryer and cook for 2–3 more minutes.

7. When the pizzas are cooked, carefully remove them from the air fryer using tongs and serve immediately. The air fryer will be hot, so ask an adult for help here if you need it.

Warning! When using a premade pizza sauce, make sure to check for any allergens in the ingredients list that you or any of your friends might need to avoid.

TUNA MELTS

SERVES 2 | TAKES 15 MINUTES

Melty cheese and savoury tuna make perfect partners between crunchy, buttery slices of bread.

INGREDIENTS:

1 x 145 g tin tuna, drained

2 tbsp mayonnaise

½ tsp lemon juice

1 spring onion, chopped

4 thick slices of bread

Butter

A pinch of salt

A grind of black pepper

60 g cheese, grated

1 Add the tuna, mayonnaise and lemon juice to a medium bowl and mix together until it is fully combined. Stir in the chopped spring onion.

2 Butter one side of each slice of bread. Place two slices of bread, butter side down, onto a plate. The butter will go on the outside of these sandwiches. Put the other two slices to one side.

3 Preheat the air fryer to 200°C/400°F.

4 Spread half of the tuna mixture onto each of the two slices of bread. Sprinkle a little salt and pepper on top of the tuna.

5 Divide the cheese between the two slices so that there is an equal amount on each one. To complete the sandwiches, place the remaining two slices of bread, butter side up, on top of the cheese.

6 Carefully place the sandwiches into the basket of the air fryer. You may need to work in batches. The air fryer will be hot, so ask an adult for help here if you need it. Set the timer to 6 minutes.

7 When the time is up, open the fryer and carefully use tongs or a spatula to turn the sandwiches over. Again, ask an adult for help here if you need it. Set the timer to 3 minutes.

8 When the time is up, open the fryer. The sandwiches should look crisp and golden. If they do not look as cooked as you would like, put them back in the air fryer for another 3 minutes before checking again.

9 Carefully remove the sandwiches from the fryer using tongs. Serve hot with a crisp, fresh salad.

CHEF IT UP!

Try adding some chopped gherkins to your tuna for a tangier taste.

SAUSAGE ROLLS

MAKES 14 SAUSAGE ROLLS | TAKES 35–45 MINUTES

Hot or cold, these sausage rolls will have you licking your fingers to scoop up every last flake of pastry.

INGREDIENTS:

1 x 320 g pack puff pastry

400 g sausage meat

2 tbsp breadcrumbs

½ small apple, grated

¼ onion, grated

½ tsp dried sage

½ tsp salt

½ tsp black pepper

1 egg, beaten

Poppy seeds or
sesame seeds

EQUIPMENT:

Rolling pin

Pastry brush

1. Add the sausage meat, breadcrumbs, grated apple, onion and seasonings to large bowl. Mix them together and put to one side. You may need to use your hands.

2. With clean dry hands, sprinkle a little flour onto a clean worktop and lay your pastry on top. Sprinkle a little more flour onto the pastry. Using a rolling pin, roll your pastry until you have a rectangle measuring 35 cm x 25 cm. Cut your rectangle in half lengthwise so that you have two long strips.

3. Use your hands to shape half of your sausage mixture into a 35 cm long sausage shape. Place your sausage in the centre of one pastry strip.

4. Use a pastry brush to paint one long edge of the pastry strip with beaten egg. Fold the other long edge of the pastry around the sausage. Then roll the pastry-wrapped sausage onto the edge with beaten egg. The egg should seal the pastry. Repeat steps 1–4 with the rest of your sausage meat and pastry.

5. Use a sharp knife to cut your super-long sausage rolls into smaller rolls measuring around 5 cm in length. Cut two slits in the top of each roll. This will help steam to escape from the sausage rolls while they are cooking. Preheat the air fryer to 200°C/400°F. While waiting for the air fryer to heat, brush each of the sausage rolls with the beaten egg and sprinkle with sesame or poppy seeds.

6. When the fryer is hot, carefully place a liner paper into the fryer basket and use tongs to carefully arrange the sausage rolls onto the paper at least 3 cm apart. Set the timer for 15 minutes. You may need to work in batches. When the time is up, the sausage rolls should be puffed up and golden. If they look a little pale, cook for another 2–4 minutes and check again.

7. If you have a meat thermometer, poke the probe of the meat thermometer into the centre of one of your sausage rolls. If the temperature of the sausage roll is 70°C/160°F or above, carefully remove them from the fryer using tongs and leave to cool on a wire rack. The air fryer will be hot, so ask an adult for help here if you need it.

8. Serve your sausage rolls hot or cold with ketchup, brown sauce or any dip you like. Yum!

CHEF IT UP!
Try spreading a layer of wholegrain mustard or chutney onto your pastry before laying on the sausage meat.

FETA FILO PARCELS

MAKES 5 PARCELS | TAKES 30 MINUTES

Crunchy, salty and just a little sweet, these feta filo parcels, or *börek*, as they are known in Turkey, are easy to make and utterly delicious. Good hot or cold, they're great for packed lunches or picnics.

INGREDIENTS:

1 x 200 g block feta cheese

5 sheets of filo pastry

4 tbsp olive oil

1 tbsp sesame seeds

2 tbsp runny honey

EQUIPMENT:

Pastry brush

1   Cut the feta cheese into five equal sticks using a table knife. Don't worry if it crumbles a bit, you can reassemble the cheese before you roll it.

2   Take one sheet of filo and lay it on a clean worktop. Use a pastry brush to spread a little olive oil all over it. Filo pastry can dry out very quickly. Cover the rest of the filo with damp pieces of kitchen roll or a clean damp tea towel. This will keep the filo moist and flexible until you are ready to use it.

3   Place a stick of feta 2–3 cm from the bottom of your oiled sheet. Fold the bottom of the sheet of pastry over the feta, and then fold in the sides.

4   Roll the feta up the sheet of pastry, making sure the sides stay tucked neatly around it. Put the roll to one side.

5   Repeat steps 2–4 for the rest of your feta sticks, making sure to cover the remaining filo with damp kitchen roll as you work.

6   Preheat the air fryer to 200°C/400°F.

7   Brush the rolls with the remaining oil and sprinkle with sesame seeds. Use tongs to place the rolls carefully into the basket of the air fryer. The air fryer will be hot, so ask an adult for help here if you need it. Set the timer to 6 minutes.

8   When the time is up, open the fryer and look at the rolls. If they look crisp and golden, use tongs to carefully remove them from the fryer. If the rolls look a little pale, set the timer to 2 minutes. Repeat until the rolls look crisp and golden.

9   Place the cooked rolls on a wire rack to cool for 5 minutes. Drizzle with honey before serving.

VG

NACHOS FOR ONE

SERVES 1 | TAKES 10 MINUTES

Why settle for a bag of tortilla chips when you could have a plate of delicious nachos? The magic of nachos is in the contrast between the warm chips covered in melty cheese, and the cool toppings.

INGREDIENTS:

30 g tortilla chips

30 g cheese, grated

1 tbsp red onion, chopped

1 tomato, sliced

EQUIPMENT:

Ovenproof dish that fits in your air fryer

Optional toppings:

1 tbsp sliced black olives

2 tbsp salsa

1 tsp chopped jalapeño chillis

1 tbsp coriander, chopped

1 tbsp sour cream

1 Preheat the air fryer to 175°C/350°F.

2 Put half of the tortilla chips into the bottom of the ovenproof dish. Top the chips with half of the cheese, half of the onions and half of the tomato.

3 Pour the rest of the chips on top of the cheese, onions and tomato. Top them with the rest of the onions, tomato and cheese.

4 Carefully put the dish into the basket of your air fryer. Set the timer to 5 minutes.

5 When the time is up, carefully remove the dish from the fryer using oven gloves.

6 Carefully remove the nachos from the dish using tongs or a spoon and place them into a bowl.

7 Add your toppings. Serve while still hot!

Layer a few tablespoons of cooked minced beef or shredded chicken in the basket of your air fryer between the chips and the cheese for a more substantial meal. `

CHEF IT UP!

Be creative! Add whatever toppings you like to your nachos.

38

DINNER

SUBTLY SPICED BEAN BURGERS

MAKES 4 BURGERS | TAKES 20 MINUTES

Not just for vegetarians, these spicy bean burgers have as much, if not more, flavour than beef burgers, and are quicker and easier to make.

INGREDIENTS:

1 x 400 g tin kidney beans or black beans

25 g rolled oats

25 g breadcrumbs

¼ medium onion, grated

½ tsp garlic powder

1 tsp cumin

½ tsp smoked paprika

1 egg, beaten

1 tbsp tomato ketchup

1 tbsp soy sauce

Oil spray

TO SERVE:

4 burger buns, sliced in half

Lettuce, cheese, tomato and onion slices

EQUIPMENT:

Potato masher

1 Preheat the air fryer to 200°C/400°F.

2 Drain the beans over the sink using a colander. Rinse the beans thoroughly with water. Tip them into a medium bowl and pat them dry using a piece of paper towel.

3 Use a potato masher to crush the beans. They don't need to be smashed to smithereens, a few half or whole beans here and there will give the burgers a nice texture.

4 Add the oats, breadcrumbs and grated onion to the beans and mix with a wooden spoon.

5 Add the garlic powder, cumin, smoked paprika, ketchup, soy sauce and beaten egg to the bowl and mix until well combined.

6 Divide the mixture into four, and shape each one into a burger using your hands. The mixture is a bit wet, so don't worry if they don't look perfect. They will still be very tasty and be hidden by the bun.

7 Carefully place a liner paper into the basket of the air fryer and use tongs or a spatula to carefully arrange the burgers on top. Try to leave 5 cm around each burger. You may need to work in batches. Store the remaining burgers in the fridge until you are ready to air fry them.

8 Spritz the top of each of the burgers with a little oil. Set the timer to 12 minutes.

9   When the time is up, open the fryer. Carefully turn the burgers over using a spatula. Set the timer to 3 minutes. While your burgers cook, gather the toppings.

10   When the time is up, carefully remove the burgers from the air fryer using a spatula and put them on a plate. The air fryer will be hot, so ask an adult for help here if you need it.

11   Carefully place the buns open side up into the basket of the air fryer. Set the temperature to 200°C/400°C and the time to 3 minutes.

12   While the buns toast, place a slice of cheese on top of each burger. The heat from the burgers will start to melt the cheese.

13   When the time is up, carefully remove the buns from the fryer using tongs. The air fryer will be hot, so ask an adult for help here if you need it.

14   To assemble your burgers, place one half of the bun onto a plate. Place a burger and your favorite toppings onto the bun, in whatever order you like. Place the other half of the burger bun on top. Repeat for the rest of your burgers.

15   Serve immediately either on their own, or perhaps with some corn cobs (see page 70) or potato wedges (see page 63).

How do you top that? Any way you like. Cool slices of avocado, a pile of tangy gherkin slices, sharp onions, or maybe just a blob of ketchup – classic.

CHEF IT UP!

Mix up your spices! Try replacing the smoked paprika and hot sauce with curry powder.

SALMON TERIYAKI

SERVES 4 |
TAKES 30 MINUTES, PLUS 1–2 HOURS FOR MARINATING

This Asian-inspired dish is super easy and super tasty, as well as being healthy. It's a total winner!

INGREDIENTS:

450 g or 4 fillets of skinned salmon

1 tsp garlic powder

1 tsp ground ginger

120 ml dark soy sauce

1 tbsp rice vinegar

1 tsp sesame oil

2 tbsp honey

1 red chilli, deseeded and diced

Fresh coriander for garnish

EQUIPMENT:

Pastry brush

4 small wooden or metal skewers

No skewers? No worries! Keep your salmon fillets whole and increase the cooking time to 6 minutes on each side.

1. Use a sharp knife to carefully cut the salmon fillets into bite-sized chunks measuring approximately 3 cm x 3 cm.

2. Add the garlic powder, ginger, soy sauce, rice vinegar, sesame oil, honey and red chilli to a medium-sized bowl. Mix the ingredients together thoroughly using a fork so that the honey is dissolved.

3. Add the salmon to the bowl and stir gently. Make sure all the pieces are coated in the marinade. Cover the bowl and put it in the fridge for 1–2 hours.

4. When it's time to cook, remove the bowl from the fridge and uncover it. Remove one piece of salmon from the bowl using your fingers, and thread it onto one of your skewers. Repeat with another piece of salmon, pushing it until it touches the first. Keep going until you've put a quarter of the salmon pieces on the skewer.

5. Repeat step 4 for each of your skewers. Try to put the same number of salmon pieces on each one and don't worry if the skewers are not full. Put the marinade to one side.

6. Preheat the air fryer to 200°C/400°F. When it has preheated, carefully put your skewers into the air fryer basket using tongs. Set the timer for 4 minutes.

7. When the time is up, open the air fryer and use tongs to carefully turn the skewers over. Use a pastry brush to carefully brush some of the leftover marinade onto each skewer. Set the timer for another 3 minutes.

8. When the time is up, carefully remove the salmon skewers from the fryer using tongs. The air fryer will be hot, so ask an adult for help here if you need it. Garnish with fresh coriander and serve immediately with rice and a green salad.

Warning! When handling fresh chillis make sure to wash your hands thoroughly afterwards before touching anything else, especially your face and eyes.

CHEF IT UP!

Replace the garlic powder and ground ginger with 2 cloves of fresh garlic and a 2.5 cm piece of fresh ginger.

SOUTHERN FRIED CHICKEN STRIPS

SERVES 2 | TAKES 35–45 MINUTES, PLUS 2–4 HOURS FOR MARINATING

These crispy chicken strips will have your family licking their plates clean. The buttermilk helps to keep the chicken succulent and moist on the inside.

INGREDIENTS:

240 ml buttermilk

350 g chicken breast, cut into strips

120 g plain flour

2 tbsp cornflour

1 tsp baking powder

1 tsp cumin

1 tsp garlic powder

1 tsp mustard powder

1 tsp onion powder

1 tsp cayenne pepper

1 tsp ground black pepper

1 tsp salt

1 egg

Oil spray

EQUIPMENT:

Sealable plastic bag

A meat thermometer (optional)

1. Pour the buttermilk into a medium sized bowl and add the chicken. Turn the chicken strips in the bowl to make sure they are coated in the buttermilk.

2. Cover the bowl and put in the fridge for 2–4 hours. Your chicken will taste better the longer you leave it in the buttermilk, but if you can't wait that long, 15–30 minutes will be fine.

3. Add the flour, cornflour, baking powder, spices and salt to a plastic bag. Seal the bag and give it a good shake.

4. Lay two pieces of kitchen paper on a plate. Take the chicken out of the fridge and uncover the bowl. Remove the chicken from the bowl and lay each piece on the paper towel. With another piece of paper towel, pat the chicken as dry as you can. Drying the chicken now will make a crispier finish later.

5. Once the chicken strips are dry, put them into the bag with the flour and spices. Seal the bag and give it a shake to cover the chicken in flour.

6. Remove the chicken strips from the bag and put them onto the plate. Crack the egg into a shallow bowl and beat with a fork. Dip each of the flour-covered chicken pieces into the beaten egg. Make sure they are completely coated, then shake off any excess.

7   Return your egg-dipped chicken to the bag containing the flour and spices. Give the bag a shake. Remove the chicken from the bag and put it back onto the plate.

8   While the strips are on the plate, spray them with a little oil. Turn them over and spray them on the other side. The oil will help the crunchy coating to turn golden brown and get super crispy.

9   Put your strips into the basket of your air fryer, making sure that they are at least 3 cm apart. You may need to work in batches. Set the air fryer to 200°C/400°F and the timer to 15 minutes.

10   When the time is up, open the fryer. The chicken should look crispy and golden. The chicken should be cooked through and very hot. Use a meat thermometer if you have one. Chicken that is cooked through should be 75°C/165°F inside. If the chicken looks a little pale, cook for another 3 minutes and check again.

11   Carefully remove the chicken from the fryer using tongs and place it on a plate. The air fryer will be hot, so ask an adult for help at this stage if you need it.

12   If cooking the chicken in batches, place the chicken onto a baking tray and keep warm in an oven set to 60°C/140°F. Use oven gloves when removing the baking tray from the oven.

13   Serve hot, with some cool, tangy coleslaw or potato salad.

Want to skip the buttermilk? An acid called lactic acid in the buttermilk helps to make the chicken tender. If you can't find any or can't get to the shops, try using milk with a teaspoon of lemon juice or vinegar stirred in instead. You can skip it completely, but your strips won't be quite as tender.

What about drumsticks and thighs? This recipe works well with drumstick and thighs, too. Increase the cooking time to 30 minutes.

PRAWN FAJITAS

SERVES 4 | TAKES 20-25 MINUTES

There is nothing like the thrill of a sizzling platter of fajitas being placed in front of you at a restaurant. While these may not sizzle, they taste just as good and can be enjoyed at home.

INGREDIENTS:

400 g raw prawns, if frozen, thawed

2 peppers, deseeded and sliced into 1 cm wide strips

1 small onion, sliced

1 tbsp oil

For the seasoning:

½ tsp paprika

½ tsp sugar

½ tsp salt

½ tsp onion powder

½ tsp garlic powder

½ tsp ground cumin

½ tsp ground black pepper

TO SERVE:

4 flour tortillas

4 wedges of lime

4 tbsp soured cream

1 Gather all the ingredients together before you start. These fajitas cook quickly, so you don't want to be running around trying to thaw prawns when your vegetables are already done.

2 Preheat the air fryer to 200°C/400°F.

3 Add all the seasoning ingredients to a small bowl and mix well using a spoon.

4 Add the peppers and the onions to a medium sized bowl and stir. Add half a tablespoon of the oil and half of the seasoning. Toss the vegetables in the seasoning and oil until they are coated thoroughly.

5 Carefully add the vegetables to the basket of your air fryer. You may need to do this in batches. Set the timer to 4 minutes.

6 While the vegetables are cooking, add the prawns to a medium sized bowl, the bowl you used earlier for the vegetables is fine. Add the rest of the seasoning and half a tablespoon of oil and toss together.

7 When time is up, open your fryer. Carefully move your vegetables to one side of the basket using tongs. The air fryer will be hot, so ask an adult for help here if you need it.

8 Arrange the prawns on the other side of the basket, approximately 2 cm apart. If you need to work in batches, remove half of your vegetables at this point and only add half of the prawns. Set the timer to 4 minutes.

9 When the time is up, open the fryer and use a pair of tongs to carefully turn over each of the prawns and give the vegetables a stir. Close the fryer and cook for 3 minutes.

10 While the fajitas are cooking, place a piece of damp kitchen roll onto a plate and place the pile of flour tortillas on top. Cover with another piece of damp kitchen roll. Put the plate in the microwave and cook on high for 30 seconds.

11 When the time is up, open the fryer. The prawns should be pink and opaque, with no blue-grey translucent parts showing. If the prawns are not fully cooked, cook for another 2–3 minutes.

12 When the prawns are done, remove the basket from your fryer and use a large spoon to put the prawns and veg onto a plate. If working in batches, place the plate into an oven set to 100°C/210°F to keep warm. Make sure to use oven gloves when removing the plate from the oven. Carefully arrange the rest of the prawns and the vegetables you put to one side in the basket of your fryer and repeat steps 8–9.

13 Serve your fajitas hot. Allow your guests to load their own tortillas with prawns and vegetables, a squeeze of lime and dollop of sour cream. Yum!

JUICY BEEF BURGERS

MAKES 4 BURGERS | TAKES 30–35 MINUTES

Burgers might taste best when cooked on the barbeque, but these air-fried patties are the next best thing.

INGREDIENTS:

500 g minced beef

1 tsp onion powder

½ tsp garlic powder

½ tsp salt

½ tsp ground black pepper

4 slices cheddar cheese

TO SERVE:

4 hamburger buns

4 slices of gherkin (optional)

4 lettuce leaves

1 tomato, sliced

EQUIPMENT:

Meat thermometer (optional)

1. Add the beef, onion powder, garlic powder, salt and black pepper to a medium sized bowl. Mix the ingredients together. You will need to use your hands in the next step, so you might as well use them now to make sure that the ingredients are thoroughly combined.

2. Use your hands to divide the beef mixture and shape it into 4 equally sized balls.

3. Squash each ball between the palms of your hands to form them into discs. Each disc should be approximately 1.5–2 cm thick. The burgers will constrict a little in the fryers which will make them smaller and fatter, so it is best to start with them a little thinner than you would like.

4. Put the discs onto a plate and chill in the fridge for 5 minutes. Wash your hands before you touch anything else.

5. Preheat the air fryer to 200°C/400°F. When the fryer is hot, carefully place a liner into the basket of the fryer. This will help to keep your basket clean.

6. Use tongs to carefully arrange the burgers on the liner paper 3–4 cm apart. You may need to work in batches. Close the fryer and set the timer to 8 minutes.

7. When the time is up, open the fryer. Carefully turn the burgers over using tongs. Set the timer to 4 minutes.

8. While the burgers are cooking, prepare your buns by carefully slicing them in half using a bread knife.

9. When the time is up, open your fryer. Your burgers should be brown and juicy, with no pink bits visible. If you are not sure if they are cooked through, either use a table knife to carefully look inside one, or if you have a meat thermometer, push the probe of it into the centre of one of your burgers. For a well-done burger, the temperature should be around 70°C/160°F. If the burgers are not cooked, close the fryer and cook for another 2 minutes before checking again.

10. When the burgers are done, open the fryer and carefully place one slice of cheddar cheese onto each burger. Close the fryer and cook for 1–2 minutes to melt the cheese.

11 When the time is up, carefully remove the burgers from the fryer using tongs and put them on a plate covered in a piece of kitchen roll. The kitchen roll will absorb any excess fat from the burgers. The air fryer will be hot, so ask an adult for help here if you need it.

12 To warm your buns (optional), carefully place them open side up into your fryer basket. Set the fryer to 180°C/350°F and the timer to 2 minutes.

13 When the time is up, carefully remove the buns from the fryer using tongs.

14 To assemble your burgers, place a bottom half of a bun on each plate. Use tongs to place a burger onto each bun. Add 1 slice of tomato, a slice of gherkin and a lettuce leaf onto each burger and then put on the top half of the bun.

15 Serve with potato wedges (see page 63) and your favourite sauces.

If adding fresh garlic, make sure to crush it or grate it before adding it to the beef. If using fresh onion, make sure to chop it very finely, or grate it. A lot of people don't like finding big bits in their burgers.

CHEF IT UP!

Use fresh garlic and onion instead of powder, for a fresher taste!

FISH GOUJONS

MAKES 6 GOUJONS | TAKES 30 MINUTES

These easy-to-make goujons are so delicious that that they could easily become a regular dinner at home.

INGREDIENTS:

450 g cod fillet

50 g plain flour

1 egg

70 g breadcrumbs

½ tsp salt

½ tsp ground black pepper

½ tsp paprika

Oil spray

1. Use a sharp knife and a cutting board to carefully cut the cod fillets into strips. The strips should be 2–3 cm wide and no longer than the basket of your fryer. After cutting, dry the cod strips by patting them with a piece of kitchen paper.

2. Add the flour, salt, pepper and paprika into a bowl and stir.

3. Crack the egg into a second bowl and beat with a fork until the white and yolk are combined.

4. Put the breadcrumbs onto a plate.

5. Drop a cod strip into the seasoned flour and turn it until it is completely covered. When the strip has been coated in flour, dip it into the bowl with the egg. The flour will help the egg to stick to the fish. Once the strip is coated in egg, press it onto the plate of breadcrumbs. The egg will help to stick the breadcrumbs to the fish. Put the breadcrumbed cod strip on a plate to one side. Repeat with the rest of the strips.

6. Preheat the air fryer to 210°C/410°F. While it is heating, spray the fish goujons with a little oil. Turn the strips and spray the other side. The oil will help the strips crisp and turn golden.

7. When the fryer is hot, carefully place a paper liner into the basket of your fryer, then carefully add the strips to the basket using tongs. Make sure none of the fish strips are touching one another. You may need to work in batches. Set the timer to 6 minutes.

8. When the time is up, open the fryer and carefully turn over your fish goujons using tongs. Close the fryer and cook for another 6 minutes.

9. When the time is up, open the fryer and look at your strips. If they look crisp and golden, carefully remove them from the fryer one by one using a pair of tongs. The air fryer will be hot, so ask an adult for help here if you need it. Place them onto a plate lined with kitchen roll.

10. If the strips look a little pale, and not as crisp as you would like, put them back into the fryer and cook for another 2–3 minutes.

11. Serve hot with wedges (see page 63) and a lemon wedge or baked beans.

STUFFED PEPPERS

SERVES 2 | TAKES 30 MINUTES

Peppers are yummy cooked in the air fryer, but did you know you can cook food inside them too? See for yourself by serving up these stuffed peppers for a delicious hearty dinner.

INGREDIENTS:

4 peppers

1 medium onion, chopped

½ courgette, chopped into 1 cm cubes

2 cloves garlic, grated or crushed

2 large tomatoes, chopped

1 tsp cumin

1 tsp oregano

1 tsp smoked paprika

2 tbsp olive oil

1 tsp salt

½ can black beans, drained and rinsed

200 g cooked rice

60 g cheddar cheese, grated

1. Heat the oil in a large frying pan over a medium heat. Carefully add the onion and cook for 3 minutes until starting to soften. Add the garlic and chopped courgette and cook for another 5 minutes.

2. Add the chopped tomatoes, cumin, oregano, smoked paprika and salt and stir. Cover the pan with a lid and turn down the heat. Leave to cook covered for 5 minutes.

3. After 5 minutes, remove the lid. Squash the tomatoes using a wooden spoon to release some of the juice, before adding the black beans and cooked rice. Cook for another 5 minutes, stirring occasionally, then remove the pan from the heat. If you notice the rice sticking to the bottom of the pan, add a little water.

4. Preheat the air fryer to 200°C/400°F.

5. Use a sharp knife and a cutting board to carefully cut the top 2–3 cm off each of the peppers. Scrape the seeds and any of the white pith out of both the tops and the bottoms of the peppers using a spoon.

6. Stand the peppers up on a plate. Carefully spoon the warm filling into the peppers. Use the back of the spoon to push the mixture down to make sure it gets into all the nooks and crannies of the pepper. Sprinkle on the cheese, before sitting the tops back on the peppers.

7. Carefully place the peppers into the basket of the air fryer using tongs. Set the timer to 15 minutes.

8. When the time is up, open the fryer. The tops of the peppers should be slightly blackened. Using tongs, carefully lift off the tops of the peppers – the cheese should look melted. If the peppers don't look as done as you would like, put the tops back on the peppers, close the fryer and cook for another 3–5 minutes before checking again.

9. Carefully remove the peppers from the fryer using tongs and leave to cool for a few minutes. The air fryer will be hot, so ask an adult for help here if you need it. Serve warm.

If you don't like the sound of these stuffed peppers, or fancy something a little different, replace the cumin and smoked paprika with the zest and juice of half a lemon and swap the cheddar for feta.

VG GF

ROASTED VEG SALAD

SERVES 1 AS A MAIN, 2 AS A SIDE DISH | TAKES 25 MINUTES

Air frying vegetables brings out their sweetness and gives them a delicious roasted flavour. Add a little dressing and a few crumbles of feta cheese, and you have a fresh tasting lunch in minutes.

INGREDIENTS:

½ onion

½ courgette

½ aubergine

½ pepper

½ tsp oregano

A few grinds of black pepper

1 tbsp olive oil

50 g feta cheese, broken into pieces

A handful of chopped parsley

Dressing:

1 tbsp extra virgin olive oil

1 tsp red wine vinegar

¼ tsp Dijon mustard

A pinch of salt

A few grinds of black pepper

1 Preheat the air fryer to 200°C/400°F.

2 Add the oil, oregano and a few grinds of black pepper to a large bowl. Put the bowl to one side.

3 Remove any peel from the onion half. Use a sharp knife to carefully cut off any papery stem from the onion, and cut off the root. Cut the onion into 2 cm thick slices. Put the slices into the bowl with the oil.

4 Cut the stems off the aubergine and courgette halves. Cut them in half again lengthways. Cut the halves into 2 cm chunks. Put the chunks into the large bowl with the onion.

5 Cut the stem off the pepper. Use a spoon to remove the seeds and scrape away any of the white parts inside the pepper. You can use a knife, but a spoon is less fiddly, and you waste less of the pepper. It doesn't matter if some seeds or white parts remain. Cut the pepper into 2 cm wide slices and then cut those slices in half. Put them into the bowl with the rest of the vegetables.

6 Toss the vegetables in the oil. Tongs are good for this if you don't want to get your hands greasy.

7 Tip the vegetables into the basket of the air fryer. Set the timer to 10 minutes.

8 While the vegetables are cooking, add the extra virgin olive oil, vinegar and mustard to a small bowl and stir with a teaspoon. Add a pinch of salt and a grind of black pepper and stir again.

9 When the time is up, open the fryer and use tongs to toss the vegetables in the basket. Close the fryer and set the timer to 5 minutes.

10 When the time is up, open the fryer. The vegetables should look brighter in colour and have a few slightly charred edges. Use a fork to prod a piece of courgette. It should be soft and not raw. If the vegetables are not as done as you would like, close the air fryer, and cook for another 2–3 minutes before checking again.

11 When the vegetables are done, carefully use tongs to put them into a large bowl. The air fryer will be hot, so ask an adult for help here if you need it. Add the dressing. Toss the vegetables in the dressing until they are well coated.

12 Tip the dressed vegetables onto a plate. Crumble over the feta cheese and add a handful of chopped parsley. Serve by themselves or with a piece of crusty bread.

Experiment with different vegetables, herbs, dressings and cheeses.

CHEF IT UP!

Cubes of butternut squash taste delicious roasted with sage!

CRISPY TOFU BOWL

SERVES 4 | TAKES 30–45 MINUTES

The secret to air frying crispy, tasty tofu is making sure you remove as much moisture from the tofu before you start.

INGREDIENTS:

300 g extra firm tofu

3 tbsp soy sauce

1 clove of garlic, grated

2 cm piece of ginger, grated

3 tbsp cornflour

Oil spray

For the sauce:

1 tsp vegetable oil

2 cloves garlic, minced or grated

2 cm piece of ginger, grated

1 tsp sesame oil

4 tbsp soy sauce

1 tbsp honey

TO SERVE:

500 g rice, cooked

300 g broccoli, steamed

1 tsp sesame seeds

1   Drain any liquid from the tofu and cut the block into 2 cm cubes. Place a piece of kitchen roll on a plate. Arrange the cubes on the piece of kitchen roll and place another piece of kitchen roll on top. Leave the tofu for 10 minutes.

2   Meanwhile, add the garlic, ginger and soy sauce to a medium bowl and mix it together with a spoon.

3   Add the cornflour to another medium bowl.

4   After 10 minutes, replace the top piece of kitchen roll with a fresh piece. Press lightly onto the kitchen roll to squeeze out any moisture.

5   Preheat the air fryer to 200°C/400°F.

6   Tip the tofu into the bowl with the soy sauce mixture. Toss the tofu in the mixture until it is well covered. Using a plastic container with a lid that seals well works here, you can put the lid on and give it a shake!

7   Remove the pieces of tofu from the bowl using tongs and put them into the bowl with the cornflour. Toss the tofu in the cornflour until it is well covered. Again, a plastic container with a lid would work well for this step.

8   Use tongs to carefully arrange the tofu pieces in the basket of your air fryer. Try to leave a few centimetres around each piece of tofu to allow air to circulate. Spray the tofu with a little oil. Set the timer to 10 minutes.

9   When the time is up, open the fryer and carefully turn over the pieces of tofu using tongs. Spritz with a little more oil. Set the timer to 10 minutes.

10 While the tofu is cooking, prepare your sauce. Start by heating 1 teaspoon of oil in a frying pan over a medium heat. Carefully add the garlic and ginger and cook for 2–3 minutes until soft and starting to brown.

11 Add the soy sauce, honey and sesame oil and stir well. Turn off the heat and cover with a lid to keep warm until the tofu is done.

12 When the time on the air fryer is up, open the fryer. The tofu should look crunchy and deep brown in colour. If it isn't as cooked as you would like, cook for another 2–3 minutes before checking again.

13 When the tofu is done, use tongs to carefully put the pieces into a bowl. The air fryer will be hot, so ask an adult for help here if you need it. Pour the sauce over the tofu and add the sesame seeds. Toss the tofu in the sauce until it is well covered.

14 To serve, spoon some cooked rice into four bowls, top each bowl with a quarter of the tofu and a few pieces of steamed broccoli.

CHEF IT UP!

Turn up the heat by adding half a teaspoon of chilli flakes to your sauce.

(VG) (GF)

JACKET POTATO

SERVES 2 | TAKES 1 HOUR

Crispy, savoury skin and fluffy on the inside, jacket potatoes with *insert your fave topping here* are the ultimate comfort food.

INGREDIENTS:

2 large potatoes, scrubbed

1 tsp olive oil

Salt

20 g cheddar cheese, grated

CHEF IT UP!

Get creative with your toppings. Cheese, beans, tuna and sweetcorn are all excellent choices!

1   Preheat the air fryer to 200°C/400°F.

2   Rub the potatoes with oil and season with a little salt. The salt will help crisp up the skin and taste delicious.

3   Use tongs to carefully put the potatoes into the basket of your air fryer. Set the timer to 45 minutes.

4   When the time is up, open the fryer. The skin of the potatoes should look crispy. To check if they are cooked through, carefully push a table knife into one of the potatoes. If the potato is cooked, the knife should slip into it easily. If the potato is not quite ready, and the knife does not go in easily, cook for another 5–10 minutes before checking again.

5   Use tongs to carefully remove the potatoes from the fryer. The air fryer will be hot, so ask an adult for help here if you need it.

6   Cut the potatoes in half both ways and serve with grated cheese on top, or any of your favourite toppings!

SIDES

VG GF

BUFFALO CAULIFLOWER 'WINGS'

SERVES 2 | TAKES 20-25 MINUTES

Unlike chicken wings, these Buffalo cauliflower wings are all bite and no bone! They pack a serious flavour punch, too. Douse your wings with as much, or as little, heat as your tastebuds can handle.

INGREDIENTS:

80 g butter, melted

4 tbsp chilli sauce (sriracha works well here)

2 tbsp honey

1 tsp garlic powder

½ tsp paprika

300 g cauliflower, broken into large florets

1–2 sticks of celery, cut into smaller sticks

For the blue cheese dip:

75 g Greek yoghurt

3 tbsp mayonnaise

30 g blue cheese, crumbled

1 tbsp lemon juice

1 tsp chives, chopped

A pinch of salt

A grind of black pepper

1 Preheat the air fryer to 220°C/430°F. If your fryer doesn't go that high, set it as hot as it will go.

2 To make the buffalo sauce, add the melted butter, chilli sauce, honey, garlic powder and paprika to a small bowl, and stir until it is all combined. Pour half of this mixture into the bottom of a large bowl.

3 Add the cauliflower to the large bowl. Gently toss the cauliflower in the sauce using tongs. This needs to be done gently to avoid breaking up the florets.

4 Carefully put a liner paper in the basket of the air fryer. Use tongs to carefully arrange the cauliflower wings on the paper. Try to leave a few centimetres around each wing to allow the air to circulate around them. You may need to work in batches.

5 Set the timer to 10 minutes. If your air fryer doesn't go to 220°C/430°F, you may need to add more time after the 10 minutes.

6 When the time is up, open the fryer and carefully turn each of the wings using tongs. Set the timer to 5 minutes.

7 While the wings are cooking, prepare your dip. Add the yoghurt, mayonnaise, salt, pepper and lemon juice to a small bowl and stir together with a spoon. Crumble in the blue cheese and chives and stir gently to combine. Don't mix it too much as it is nice for the dip to have a bit of texture.

8 When the wings are done, carefully remove them from the fryer using tongs. Let one cool slightly, and taste. How is the spice? If you think you can take a little more heat, use a pastry brush to slick a layer of the remaining sauce on the wings before arranging on the plate. This will make them sticky and extra tasty. Serve the wings hot alongside the blue cheese dip and celery sticks.

SNACKING SPROUTS

SERVES 2-4 | TAKES 15 MINUTES

These Brussels sprouts aren't the boiled green stuff of nightmare roast dinners, they are crunchy, savoury and delicious enough to be a snack all on their own.

INGREDIENTS:

400 g Brussels sprouts

1 tbsp olive oil

½ tsp salt

½ tsp black pepper

2 cloves garlic, crushed

½ tsp chilli flakes

CHEF IT UP!

Give these Brussels sprouts a Mediterranean boost: sprinkle a tablespoon of grated parmesan and a tablespoon of lemon zest.

1 Use a sharp knife to carefully cut off the stem of each of the Brussels sprouts, then cut them in half lengthways. Pull away any old-looking leaves.

2 Preheat the air fryer to 200°C/400°F.

3 Add the oil, salt, pepper, garlic and chilli flakes to a medium sized bowl. Mix the ingredients together using a fork. Add the sprout halves to the bowl and toss in the spiced oil.

4 Carefully place a liner into the basket of the air fryer. Use tongs to carefully arrange the sprouts in a single layer on the liner. You may need to work in batches. Set the timer to 5 minutes.

5 When the time is up, open the fryer and give the basket a shake to toss your sprouts. Set the timer to 5 minutes.

6 When the time is up, open the fryer. The sprouts should look crispy on the outside. Push a fork into one of the sprouts. The fork should go into the sprout easily.

7 If the sprouts are still hard inside or do not look as crispy as you would like, cook for 3 more minutes before checking again.

8 When the sprouts are ready, put a piece of kitchen roll onto a plate and carefully use a serving spoon to place the sprouts onto it. The kitchen roll will soak up any excess oil.

9 Serve the sprouts immediately, either alongside a main dish or all on their own.

(VG) (VE) (GF)

SPICY POTATO WEDGES

SERVES 2 | TAKES 25 MINUTES

Chunky wedges are a great alternative to French fries. Not only do you not have to bother with peeling them, their chunky form is ideal for scooping up your favourite dip or sauces.

INGREDIENTS:

2 large potatoes, cleaned

2 tbsp olive oil

1 tsp salt

1 tsp ground black pepper

½ tsp garlic powder

½ tsp paprika

1. Carefully cut the potatoes in half lengthways using a sharp knife and a cutting board. Put one half of the potato onto the board, cut-side down, and cut it in half again to make two quarters. Turn one of the quarters so that its skin is on the board, and cut in half lengthways again to make two eighths. Repeat this with the rest of the potato to give you 16 wedges.

2. Preheat the air fryer to 220°C/430°F.

3. Pour the olive oil into a large bowl. Add the salt, pepper, garlic powder and paprika and mix well.

4. Add your wedges to the bowl and toss them in the mixture until they are coated with oil and spices.

5. When the fryer is hot, open it and use tongs to carefully arrange the wedges carefully in the basket. Try to make sure none of the wedges are touching to allow the air to circulate around them. You may need to work in batches.

6. Set the timer for 10 minutes.

7. When the time is up, open the fryer and carefully turn your wedges using a pair of tongs. The air fryer will be hot, so ask an adult for help here if you need it. Close the fryer and cook for a further 7 minutes.

8. When the time is up, open the fryer. The wedges should look crispy and golden. If they still look a little pale, or you would prefer them to be crispier, cook for another 2–3 minutes.

9. Carefully remove the wedges from the fryer using tongs and place them on a plate covered in kitchen roll.

10. Serve warm either on their own, or alongside your favourite burger (see pages 40 and 48).

(VG) (VE) (GF)

SNACK PEAS

SERVES 2 | TAKES 40 MINUTES

These sweet and smoky flavoured chickpeas are finger-licking good!

INGREDIENTS:

1 tin chickpeas

2 tsp olive oil

1 tsp chilli powder

1 tsp caster sugar

1 tsp onion powder

½ tsp smoked paprika

½ tsp salt

1. Drain the can of chickpeas using a colander. Lay three sheets of kitchen roll on your worktop. Carefully pour the chickpeas onto the kitchen roll and spread them out. Use another piece of kitchen roll to pat the chickpeas dry.

2. Preheat the air fryer to 160°C/320°F.

3. Tip the chickpeas into a bowl and add the oil. Toss the chickpeas in the oil until they are covered evenly.

4. Once the air fryer has preheated, carefully pour the chickpeas into the basket. Shake the basket to spread them out, and put it into the fryer. Set the timer for 30 minutes.

5. While your chickpeas are cooking, add the chilli powder, onion powder, smoked paprika, salt and sugar to a clean bowl and mix thoroughly.

6. When the time is up, open the air fryer and carefully remove one of the chickpeas using tongs and wait a minute for it to cool. Taste the chickpea. If it is still soft inside, cook the chickpeas for another 3–4 minutes and check again. If the chickpea is crunchy all the way through, remove the basket from the fryer and carefully use a serving spoon to put the hot chickpeas into the bowl of spice mix.

7. Toss the chickpeas in the spice mix with a spoon until they are evenly coated. Serve warm or cool!

Missing any of the spices? Experiment with what you have! Dried basil, oregano, rosemary, lemon zest or parmesan cheese would be great, too! Or why not make a sweet treat using cinnamon and sugar?

TORTILLA CHIPS

SERVES 2 | TAKES 5-10 MINUTES

Tortilla chips are tasty, but hot, fresh tortilla chips are next-level dee-licious. Serve these with your favourite dips, or why not try pairing with the roasted tomato salsa on page 66?

INGREDIENTS:

4 tortilla wraps

½ tsp salt

Oil spray

1 Cut each tortilla in half using kitchen scissors, then cut each half into three triangles.

2 Spray the triangles with oil and turn them over to spray on the other side.

3 Set the air fryer to preheat to 180°C/350°F.

4 Once it has preheated, carefully spread your chips in a single layer in the basket using tongs. Set the timer for 3 minutes.

5 When the time is up, open your air fryer and carefully turn your chips using tongs. Close your fryer and cook for another 1–2 minutes.

6 When the chips are done, remove them from the fryer using tongs. The air fryer will be hot, so ask an adult for help here if you need it.

7 Sprinkle the chips with salt and serve warm.

CHEF IT UP!

Inject some extra flavour into your chips by squeezing a little lime juice onto them before serving!

VG VE GF

ROASTED TOMATO SALSA

SERVES 4 | TAKES 30 MINUTES

This fresh-tasting salsa is the perfect dip to go with your favourite chips, whether they are from a shop or homemade (see page 65).

INGREDIENTS:

1 tbsp olive oil

4 large tomatoes, halved

1 small onion, cut into quarters

4 cloves garlic, peeled

1 fresh jalapeño chilli pepper

Salt

Pepper

Tortilla chips

Be aware that this salsa is gluten free, but tortilla chips will add gluten.

1 Preheat the air fryer to 200°C/400°F.

2 Pour 1 tablespoon of olive oil into a large bowl. Add the tomatoes, onion and garlic to the bowl and toss in the oil. Do this gently so as not to break up the onion quarters too much.

3 When the fryer has preheated, carefully place a liner paper into the basket. Use tongs to carefully place the halved tomatoes onto the paper skin-side down, then add the onion and garlic cloves. Try to leave a little space around each item to allow the heat to circulate. You may need to work in batches if your fryer is not big enough to fit everything. Set the timer for 10 minutes.

4 Meanwhile, prepare the chilli pepper by cutting off the stem and then cutting it in half lengthwise. Scrape out the seeds using a teaspoon. These can be thrown away.

5 When the time is up, open the fryer and use tongs to carefully add the chilli pepper halves, skin side down, to the basket. Set the timer for 5 minutes.

6 When the time is up, open the fryer. The onions should have softened slightly and be a little blackened around the edges. Use tongs to carefully transfer your ingredients from the frier to a large bowl and leave to cool for 5–10 minutes. The air fryer will be hot, so ask an adult for help here if you need it.

7 When the ingredients have cooled slightly, roughly chop them in the bowl using a pair of kitchen scissors. Keep chopping until the vegetables are broken up into approximately 1 cm chunks, paying extra attention to the chilli. It will be a bit sloppy so there is no way to be exact. Use a tortilla chip to sample your salsa, then add salt and pepper to suit your taste.

8 For a smoother salsa, ask an adult to help you use a hand blender. Submerge the blender in the bowl and switch it on for 2–3 seconds. Keep the blender submerged, otherwise salsa will fly everywhere! Repeat this step until your salsa is as smooth as you want it to be.

Warning! Make sure to wash your hands thoroughly after handling chillis. Touching chillis and then touching your eyes can hurt a lot. If this happens, rinse with plenty of water.

CHEF IT UP!

Add a squeeze of fresh lime juice and a handful of chopped coriander before serving.

HALLOUMI FRIES

MAKES 8 FRIES | TAKES 25 MINUTES

Halloumi is a cheese that originates from Cyprus. Halloumi is a perfect cheese for air frying because it can be cooked at high temperatures without turning into a melty mess. Try these crunchy, salty, squeaky halloumi fries with your favourite sweet or spicy chilli sauce.

INGREDIENTS:

225 g halloumi

30 g plain flour

½ tsp oregano

½ tsp garlic powder

½ tsp ground black pepper

1 egg

Oil spray

50 g breadcrumbs

Out of breadcrumbs? No problem, crush up a handful of your favourite savoury crackers and use them instead.

CHEF IT UP!

Experiment with different herbs and spices in your dipping flour.

1 Use a table knife to cut the block of halloumi into 1.5 cm thick strips, or fries. Pat the strips dry using kitchen paper and put to one side.

2 Add the flour, oregano, garlic powder and black pepper onto a plate and mix together thoroughly. Add breadcrumbs to a second plate and place a sheet of kitchen paper onto a third plate. Finally, crack the egg into a medium sized bowl and beat with a fork until the white and yolk are combined.

3 Working one at a time, place the halloumi fries in the seasoned flour and make sure each fry is covered. Then dip the floured fries into the bowl with the beaten egg. The flour helps the egg to stick.

4 Place the eggy fries onto the plate with the breadcrumbs. Toss the fries in the breadcrumbs until they are fully covered. Place the breadcrumbed fries onto the plate with kitchen paper and spray both sides with oil. Preheat the air fryer to 200°C/400°F.

5 When the fryer is hot, use tongs to carefully place the fries into the basket. Make sure there is a little space around each fry so that they cook evenly. You may need to work in batches. Cook for 5 minutes then use tongs to carefully turn your fries and cook for a further 5 minutes.

6 When the time is up, open the fryer and look at your fries. If they look a little pale, cook for another 2–4 minutes, checking every minute or so until crisp and golden. When they look ready, use tongs to carefully remove them from the fryer. The air fryer will be hot, so ask an adult for help here if you need it.

7 Allow the fries to cool for a few minutes before serving with your favourite spicy dipping sauce.

HOT HONEY CORN COBS

SERVES 4 |
TAKES 25 MINUTES, PLUS 20 MINUTES COOLING TIME

These hot honey corn on the cobs are sweet, sticky and moreish. Team with a spicy creamy mayonnaise and salad to make a delicious lunch.

INGREDIENTS:

4 mini corn on the cobs
(If you can't find mini corn on the cobs, ask an adult to help you break standard corn cobs in half. You can do this before they are cooked by holding each end of the cob firmly, and snapping the cob so it breaks in the middle.)

1 tbsp oil

2 tsp honey

½ tsp paprika

½ tsp garlic powder

½ tsp salt

½ tsp black pepper

For the dip:

4 tbsp mayonnaise

½ tsp hot sauce

1 tsp lime juice

1. Add the oil, honey, paprika, garlic powder, salt and black pepper to a bowl and mix with a fork.

2. Preheat the air fryer to 200°C/400°F.

3. Use a pastry brush or spoon to coat each of the corn cobs with the spiced honey and oil.

4. Use tongs to carefully arrange the cobs in the basket of the air fryer in a single layer. You can use an air fryer liner here if you want. Set the timer to 6 minutes.

5. When the time is up, open the fryer and carefully turn each of the cobs using tongs. Set the timer to 6 minutes.

6. While they cook, add the mayonnaise, lime juice and hot sauce to a small bowl and mix.

7. When the time is up, open the fryer. The corn should look plump and juicy, and have browned in places. If the corn doesn't look as cooked as you would like, close the fryer and cook at 200°C/400°F for 3 minutes before checking again.

8. Carefully remove the cobs from the fryer using tongs. Leave to cool for a few minutes, and then serve warm with the dipping sauce.

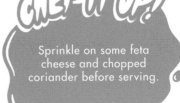

CHEF IT UP!

Sprinkle on some feta cheese and chopped coriander before serving.

GARLIC BREAD

SERVES 2 | TAKES 10 MINUTES

There are very few meals that aren't made better with a slice of garlic bread!

INGREDIENTS:

60 g butter, room temperature

4 cloves of garlic, finely grated

1 tbsp parsley, chopped

4 tbsp parmesan cheese, grated

6 slices French bread

CHEF IT UP!

For cheesier garlic bread, try adding a sprinkling of mozzarella cheese to each slice.

1 Preheat the air fryer to 175°C/350°F.

2 Add the butter, garlic and parsley to a small bowl. Stir well with a spoon.

3 Spread each slice of bread with a thick layer of garlic butter.

4 Sprinkle the parmesan cheese on top of the butter.

5 Use tongs to carefully place the slices of bread into the basket of your air fryer. Try to leave at least 3 cm around each slice. You may need to work in batches.

6 Set the timer to 5 minutes.

7 When the time is up, if the bread looks crisp around the edges and all the cheese and butter has melted, use tongs to carefully remove it from the fryer. The air fryer will be hot, so ask an adult for help at this point if you need it. If the bread looks a little pale, cook for a further 2 minutes.

8 Serve warm.

VG

PICKLE CHIPS

SERVES 2 | TAKES 20 MINUTES

Step aside, lowly onion rings, the pickle (or sliced gherkin) chip has entered the chat. Crunchy, salty and tangy fried gherkins, otherwise known as pickles in the USA, are magnificently moreish.

INGREDIENTS:

1 x 340 g jar crinkle cut/burger gherkins (about 20 round slices)

1 egg

8 tbsp dried breadcrumbs

Oil spray

1. Preheat the air fryer to 200°C/400°F.

2. Open the jar of gherkin slices and drain them using a colander. Lay the gherkin slices out on a piece of kitchen roll and pat them dry.

3. Put the breadcrumbs onto a plate. Crack the egg into a small bowl and beat it.

4. Dip each gherkin slice into the beaten egg and then into the breadcrumbs, making sure each gets a good coating. Spray your pickle chips with a little oil.

5. Use tongs to carefully arrange your chips in the basket of your air fryer. Try to leave at least 2 cm around each chip. You may need to work in batches. Set the timer to 7 minutes.

6. When the time is up, open the fryer and carefully turn each of the chips over using tongs. Set the timer to 4 minutes.

7. When the time is up, open the fryer. The chips should look crisp and golden. If they look a little pale, cook for another 2–3 minutes before checking again.

8. Carefully remove the chips from the fryer using tongs. The air fryer will be hot, so ask an adult for help here if you need it. Serve with your favourite dipping sauce.

ONION BHAJIS

MAKES 12 BHAJIS | TAKES 1 HOUR 30 MINUTES

Onion bhajis are a popular snack food enjoyed throughout India and are a favourite starter in Indian restaurants all over the United Kingdom. They are best enjoyed hot, but make great picnic snacks, too.

INGREDIENTS:

400 g onion (about 2–3 onions)

1 tsp salt

140 g gram flour

1 tsp turmeric

½ tsp garlic powder

2 cm piece of ginger, grated

½ tsp chilli powder

½ tsp cumin

A handful of chopped coriander

Lemon wedges

Oil spray

EQUIPMENT:

12 silicone muffin cases

1 Use a sharp knife to carefully cut the onion in half, through the root. Peel away the skin and throw it away. Place the onion halves flat side down and cut off the root and any papery skin around the top of the onion. Cut each half of the onion into slices about half a centimetre thick.

2 Put the onion slices into a large bowl and add the salt. Toss the onions in the salt. Leave the bowl for 1 hour.

3 Meanwhile, take a small bowl and add the flour, turmeric, garlic powder, grated ginger, chilli and cumin. Mix them together well and put to one side.

4 After 1 hour, return to the bowl. You will notice that the onions look wetter than they were when you left them. The salt has drawn out some of the water. Put your hands into the bowl and squeeze more water out of the onions. Squeeze out as much as you can. Leave the water and the onions in the bowl.

5 Add the spiced flour mixture to the onions. Stir together until all the flour is mixed in. It should look like a lumpy yellow batter. If the onion mixture looks a little dry, stir in 1 tablespoon of water at a time until it looks like a batter.

6 Preheat the air fryer to 200°C/400°F.

7 While the air fryer is heating up, spray 12 silicone muffin cases with a little oil. Scoop 2 tablespoons of the bhaji batter into each case. Spray the top of each bhaji with a little more oil.

8 When the fryer is hot, use tongs to carefully put the muffin cases into the basket of your fryer. Try to leave at least 3 cm around each muffin case. You may need to work in batches.

9 Set the timer to 10 minutes.

10 When the time is up, open the fryer. Use a pair of tongs to carefully tip each bhaji out of its muffin case into the basket of the fryer. Remove the muffin cases. The air fryer will be hot, so ask an adult for help here if you need it.

11 Set the timer to 6 minutes.

12 When the time is up, open the fryer. If the bhajis look crisp and golden, carefully remove them from the fryer using tongs and put them on a plate covered with a piece of kitchen roll. If the bhajis look a little pale, cook for another 2 minutes before checking again.

13 Arrange the bhajis on a plate and sprinkle with chopped coriander. Serve with a wedge of lemon or a cool yoghurt dip.

CHEF IT UP!
Add a chopped chilli to your batter to make it spicy. Make sure to wash your hands thoroughly after handling chillis.

GF

PIGS IN BLANKETS

MAKES 12 MINI PIGS IN BLANKETS | TAKES 20 MINUTES

Pigs in blankets, or pork sausages wrapped in bacon, are a traditional side dish served with Christmas dinner. Learn how to make your own little piggies in the air fryer and enjoy them all year round.

INGREDIENTS:

4 pork chipolata sausages

4 slices streaky bacon

EQUIPMENT:

Meat thermometer

1. Preheat the air fryer to 180°C/350°F.

2. Wrap each sausage in a piece of bacon. Use a sharp knife to carefully cut each bacon-wrapped sausage into three.

3. Use tongs to carefully place your sausages into the basket of the air fryer. Try to leave at least 3 cm around each sausage. Set the timer to 6 minutes.

4. When the time is up, open the fryer. Carefully turn the sausages over using tongs and set the timer for another 6 minutes.

5. When the time is up, open the fryer. The sausages should be brown and sizzling.

6. To tell whether they are cooked, insert a meat thermometer into the centre of one of the sausages. If the temperature reads 70°C/160°F or higher, remove them from the fryer using tongs.

7. If the temperature reads less than 70°C/160°F, cook for another 2–3 minutes before checking again.

8. Use tongs to carefully put the sausages on a plate lined with a piece of kitchen roll. The kitchen roll will absorb some of the excess fat. Serve with ketchup, gravy or your favourite dipping sauce.

CHEF IT UP!

Why stop with sausages? Lots of things are delicious wrapped in bacon, such as prawns, fish and even dried apricots!

DESSERT

LEMON DRIZZLE CUPCAKES

MAKES 6–8 CUPCAKES | TAKES 30–45 MINUTES

These sweet treats are tangy and delicious. They make your kitchen smell great, too!

INGREDIENTS:

1 large egg

70 g caster sugar

110 g plain flour

¾ tsp baking powder

50 g butter

75 ml milk

Zest of 1 lemon

1 tbsp lemon juice

For the glaze:

60 g icing sugar

3 tbsp lemon juice

EQUIPMENT:

6–8 silicone cupcake cases

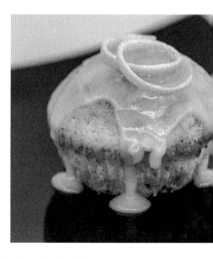

1 Crack the egg into the bowl and add the sugar, flour, lemon zest and baking powder. Whisk the ingredients together until the mixture looks like sand and then put to one side.

2 Add the milk and the butter into a microwave-safe bowl or measuring jug. Microwave the butter and milk for 30 seconds. After 30 seconds, check to see if the butter has melted. If it is still solid, return it to the microwave for another 30 seconds. Repeat until the butter has just melted. Add the lemon juice and stir with a fork to combine.

3 Pour the milk and butter into the flour mixture and whisk until smooth with no big lumps (little sandy lumps are okay).

4 Spoon the mixture into the silicone cupcake cases, filling each until it is about three quarters full.

5 Preheat the air fryer to 180°C/350°F.

6 Use tongs to carefully place the cupcakes in the air fryer basket and set the timer for 15 minutes.

7 When the time is up, check on your cupcakes. They should be risen and golden. To make extra sure they are done, insert a table knife into the centre of one of the cupcakes and pull it out. If the knife is clean when you pull it out, the cupcakes are done! If the knife has raw cake mix on it when you pull it out, put the cupcakes back in the fryer for 2–3 more minutes and then check again.

8 Use tongs to carefully remove your cupcakes from the fryer basket and place them on a wire rack to cool. The air fryer will be hot, so ask an adult for help here if you need it.

9 Put the icing sugar into a small bowl and add the lemon juice 1 tablespoon at a time. Mix together with a fork until smooth. Keep adding lemon juice until you've reached the desired consistency for your icing. For a classic lemon drizzle, it should be fairly runny. Spoon the drizzle mixture over the warm cupcakes.

10 Leave your cupcakes to cool for at least 5–10 minutes more.

BANANA NUT MUFFINS

MAKES 16–18 CUPCAKES OR 10–12 MUFFINS | TAKES 30 MINUTES

These nutty banana muffins are the perfect way to use up bananas that are looking past their best.

INGREDIENTS:

3 ripe bananas

70 g butter, melted

1 egg, beaten

100 g soft brown sugar

4 tbsp plain yoghurt

240 g flour

½ tsp cinnamon

½ tsp ground nutmeg

1 tsp baking powder

60 g chopped walnuts

EQUIPMENT:

18 silicone cupcake cases or
12 silicone muffin cases

CHEF IT UP!

Top your muffins with crushed walnuts and brown sugar before air frying to give a crunchy topping.

1. Peel the bananas and add them to a large bowl. Mash the bananas into a smooth paste using the back of a fork. Add the butter, egg, sugar and yoghurt and mix well.

2. Add the flour, spices and baking powder and mix together until there is no dry flour left in the bowl. The batter should be quite thick. Add the walnuts and stir gently so as not to break them up too much.

3. Preheat the air fryer to 175°C/350°F.

4. Spoon the mixture into the cupcake or muffin cases. Fill each case until it is about three quarters full.

5. When the fryer is hot, open the fryer and use tongs to carefully put the filled cases into the basket. Try to leave at least 3 cm around each muffin case. You may need to work in batches. Set the timer to 15 minutes for cupcakes or 18 minutes for muffins.

6. When the time is up, open the fryer. The muffins should have risen and look a deep golden brown. To check if they are done, poke a table knife into the centre of one of the muffins and pull it out. If the knife comes out with raw batter on it, cook for another 2–3 minutes before checking again. When the knife comes out clean, carefully remove the muffins from the fryer using tongs and leave them to cool on a wire rack. Serve warm or cold, or with a serving of fresh fruit to make a delicious breakfast.

Warning! This recipe contains nuts. Make sure none of your family or friends have nut allergies before sharing these muffins with them.

CHOCOLATE FONDANT LAVA CAKES

SERVES 2 | TAKES 20-25 MINUTES

In the USA, they call these gooey desserts chocolate lava cakes because they are crusty on the outside and molten in the middle, just like a volcano. They are also dangerously delicious.

INGREDIENTS:

2 medium eggs

1 tsp vanilla extract

¼ tsp salt

50 g butter, plus a little extra for greasing

125 g dark chocolate chips

25 g plain flour, plus 1 tbsp extra for dusting

EQUIPMENT:

Whisk

2 ramekins, 9 cm wide and 5 cm deep, or roughly 200 ml capacity

1. Preheat the air fryer to 180°C/350°F.

2. Dip a piece of kitchen roll in butter and rub it around the inside of both ramekins until they are thoroughly greased. Add 1 tablespoon of flour to one ramekin. Tilt and tip the ramekin so that the flour moves around and sticks to the butter. When the inside is coated in flour, tip any extra into the other ramekin and do the same. This will stop your fondants from sticking.

3. Crack the eggs into a medium-sized bowl and whisk until the whites and yolk are combined. Add the vanilla extract and whisk again.

4. Put the butter and the chocolate chips in a microwave-safe bowl or jug. Place the jug in the microwave and cook on high for 20 seconds.

5. Remove the jug from the microwave. The chocolate chips and the butter should have started to melt. Use a fork to stir them together. If, after stirring, the butter and chocolate have fully melted, skip to the next step. If they are not fully melted, return the jug to the microwave and cook on high for another 20 seconds before stirring again. Repeat until the chocolate has fully melted into the butter.

6. Carefully touch the side of the jug. The jug should feel warm, but not burning hot. If the jug is very hot, set it aside to cool for a few minutes.

7. When the jug is warm but not hot, pour about quarter of the chocolate butter mix into the bowl with the eggs and whisk until combined, before pouring in a little more and whisking again. Repeat until all the butter and chocolate is combined with the eggs.

8. Add the salt and the flour and whisk again until combined.

9. Spoon the mixture into the prepared ramekins until they are three quarters full.

10 Use tongs to carefully place the ramekins into the basket of the air fryer. Set the timer to 8 minutes.

11 When the time is up, open the fryer and look at the tops of your fondants. If the tops look dry and cooked with no visible wet/raw mixture, use a pair of oven gloves or tongs to carefully remove them from the basket. You may need to ask an adult to help you. If they look a little raw, close the fryer and cook for another 2–3 minutes before checking again.

12 Leave the fondants to cool for 5 minutes. They will continue to cook during this time.

13 After 5 minutes, run a table knife around the inside of the ramekins to loosen them.

14 To remove the fondant, carefully hold the ramekin with an oven mitt and put a plate on top of it, then turn the plate and the ramekin upside down. The ramekin might still be hot, so ask an adult for help here if you need it. Serve warm with fresh fruit.

CHEF IT UP!

Make it look professional with a dusting of icing sugar and some fresh fruit as a garnish.

Warning! If your ramekins are smaller, you will need to adjust the baking time. If you're making these for a special occasion, it might be worth doing a practice batch so you're sure on your timings.

MARSHMALLOW SLIDERS

MAKES 2 SLIDERS | TAKES 5 MINUTES

No need to wait for your next bonfire or barbeque – the tool for perfectly toasted marshmallows is right there in your kitchen.

INGREDIENTS:

4 chocolate digestive biscuits, 2 per slider

24 mini marshmallows

CHEF IT UP!

Spread a layer of peanut or almond butter on your biscuits before adding the marshmallows.

1 Preheat the air fryer to 200°C/400°F.

2 While the fryer is heating, put two of the biscuits, chocolate side up, on a plate or chopping board. Arrange 12 mini marshmallows on top of each biscuit on the plate.

3 When the fryer is hot, carefully put a liner paper into the basket of the fryer. Use tongs to carefully place the marshmallow-covered biscuits on the liner. Set the timer to 2 minutes.

4 When the time is up, open the fryer. The marshmallows should look golden and toasty, and the chocolate should look melted. If the marshmallows don't look as well done as you would like, close the fryer and cook for 1 minute before checking again.

5 Using tongs, carefully remove the biscuits from the fryer and put them on a plate. The air fryer will be hot, so ask an adult for help here if you need it.

6 To assemble the sliders, place the other two biscuits chocolate side down on top of the toasted marshmallow biscuits. The heat from the toasted marshmallows will melt the chocolate of the top biscuits. Serve right away!

Warning! If you add in peanut or almond butter, this recipe will contain nuts. Make sure none of your family or friends have nut allergies before sharing these sliders with them.

BAKED BANANA SPLIT

MAKES 2 BANANA SPLITS | TAKES 15 MINUTES

These banana splits are so delicious no one will believe how easy they are to make. Your friends and family will go bananas over them – guaranteed.

INGREDIENTS:

2 large bananas

2 tbsp chopped nuts

10 mini marshmallows

A few chocolate chips or broken pieces of dark chocolate

Ice cream to serve

CHEF IT UP!

Stuff your banana with whatever sounds good to you! Jelly beans? Peanut butter? Crushed ginger biscuits? Go for it.

1 Preheat the air fryer to 200°C/400°F.

2 Carefully, use a sharp knife to cut a deep slit all the way along the inside curve of each of the bananas. Be careful to push the knife all the way through the banana, but not through the skin on the bottom.

3 Stuff the slits of your bananas with marshmallows, chopped nuts and broken pieces of dark chocolate.

4 Stand your bananas on their uncut edge. If they won't stand up on their own, put them into an oven-safe dish that fits into your air fryer.

5 Put the bananas, with or without the dish, into the basket of the air fryer. Set the timer to 8 minutes.

6 When the time is up, open the fryer. The banana skins should have turned black and the chocolate should have melted. If the banana skins look a little yellow, cook for another 2–3 minutes.

7 Carefully remove the bananas from the fryer using tongs. The air fryer will be hot, so ask an adult for help here if you need it.

8 Serve your bananas hot, with or without a scoop of ice cream.

Warning! This recipe contains nuts. Make sure none of your family or friends have nut allergies before sharing these banana splits with them.

VG

CHOCOLATE BROWNIES

MAKES 16 BROWNIES | TAKES 25-30 MINUTES

These chocolate brownies melt in the mouth and are the perfect balance of fudgy, chewy and crunchy.

INGREDIENTS:

125 g butter, plus extra for greasing

130 g dark chocolate, broken into pieces

2 medium eggs

125 g caster sugar

½ tsp salt

80 g plain flour

30 g cocoa powder

EQUIPMENT:

Silicone spatula

Whisk

20 cm x 20 cm square tin
or casserole dish, or a tin that fits
in your air fryer

Toothpick or table knife

Baking paper

1 Before you start, check that the tin you plan to use fits inside your air fryer. Air fryers come in all shapes and sizes. If a 20 cm x 20 cm tin is too big, work in batches with 2 loaf tins, or even use silicone cupcake cases to make brownie bites.

2 If using a tin, place it onto a piece of baking paper and draw around it with a pencil. Use a pair of scissors to cut out around the line to get a piece of paper the size of your tin.

3 Dip a piece of kitchen roll into some butter and rub it all around the inside of your tin. Put the baking paper piece in the tin, on top of the greased bottom. If using cupcake cases, you can skip this step.

4 Crack your eggs into a medium bowl. Add the salt and sugar and beat with a fork.

5 Put the butter and the chocolate pieces in a microwave-safe bowl or jug. Place the jug in the microwave and cook on high for 20 seconds.

6 Remove the jug from the microwave. The chocolate chips and the butter should have started to melt. Use a fork to stir them together. If, after stirring, the butter and chocolate have fully melted, skip to the next step. If they are not fully melted, return the jug to the microwave, and cook on high for another 20 seconds before stirring again. Repeat until the chocolate has fully melted into the butter.

7 Carefully touch the side of the jug. The jug should feel warm, but not burning hot. If the jug is very hot, set it aside to cool for a few minutes.

8 When the jug is warm but not hot, pour about a quarter of the chocolate butter mix into the bowl with the eggs and whisk until combined, before pouring in a little more and whisking again. Repeat until all the butter and chocolate is combined with the eggs.

9 Add the flour and the cocoa powder and mix well until there are no dry lumps of flour. Preheat the air fryer to 160°C/320°F.

10 While the fryer heats up, pour your mixture into your prepared tin or tins. If using cupcake cases, spoon the mixture into the cases until they are three quarters full. Carefully place the tin into the air fryer, or use tongs to carefully place the silicone cases into the basket, making sure to leave 2 cm between each case.

11 Set the timer to 15 minutes (8 minutes for cupcake cases).

12 When the time is up, open the fryer. To check whether they are done, poke a toothpick or table knife into the centre of the brownies and pull it out. If it comes out with a few crumbs attached or just a bit of gooey mixture, use oven gloves to remove the brownies from the fryer and leave to cool. If it comes out with a lot of raw brownie mix on it, close the fryer. Set the timer to 3 minutes, then check again.

13 Leave the brownies to cool in the tin for 15–20 minutes.

14 When the brownies have cooled enough to handle, run a table knife around the inside of your tin and turn them out of the tin. Cut the brownies into 5 cm x 5 cm squares.

Warning! If you add in walnuts or hazelnuts, this recipe will contain nuts. Make sure none of your family or friends have nut allergies before sharing these brownies with them.

CHEF IT UP!

If you like nuts, try baking a batch with walnuts or hazelnuts. Delicious!

CHEESECAKES

MAKES 4 |
TAKES 30 MINUTES, PLUS 2-3 HOURS CHILLING TIME

These baked cheesecakes don't take a lot of work but do take a bit of time to chill. One thing is for sure, they are worth waiting for.

INGREDIENTS:

130 g digestive biscuits, plain or chocolate is fine

30 g butter, melted

280 g cream cheese, room temperature

2 eggs, beaten

3 tbsp caster sugar

1 tsp vanilla extract

EQUIPMENT:

Rolling pin

Wooden spoon or electric whisk

4 ramekins, 9 cm wide and 5 cm deep, or roughly 200 ml capacity

1. Put the biscuits into a plastic bag and crush them with a rolling pin. Empty the bag of crushed biscuits into a medium sized bowl. Add the melted butter and mix.

2. Spoon a quarter of the buttery biscuit mixture into each of your ramekins. Smooth out the mixture using the back of a metal spoon.

3. Add the cream cheese, sugar, vanilla and eggs to a large bowl. Mix them together thoroughly using a wooden spoon. You can use an electric whisk if you have one. Spoon an equal quantity of the cheese mixture into each ramekin.

4. Preheat the air fryer to 155°C/310°F.

5. Cover each of the ramekins with a piece of tin foil. Fold the foil over the sides and crimp around the edges to keep it in place. Poke holes in the foil with a fork or toothpick.

6. Carefully place the ramekins into the basket of the air fryer using tongs. Set the timer to 25 minutes.

7. When the time is up, carefully remove one of the cheesecakes from the fryer using tongs or oven gloves. The air fryer will be hot, so ask an adult for help here if you need it.

8. Carefully remove the foil. The cheesecake should look as though it has set with no liquid visible. If the cheesecake looks a little wet, carefully cover it again with the foil and return it to the fryer using tongs or oven gloves. Cook for another 2–3 minutes before checking again.

9. When they are done, remove the cheesecakes from the fryer and leave them to cool. This will take 2–3 hours. For best result, put the cheesecakes in the fridge overnight once they have cooled down from the air fryer. Serve with fresh fruit, a sprig of mint and a dusting of icing sugar.

Ginger biscuits are a spicy choice and work well with a little lime zest in the cream cheese mix, instead of vanilla.

BERRY CRUMBLES

SERVES 2 | TAKES 15 MINUTES

Fruit crumble is a classic dessert! Make your own in a matter of minutes with this easy recipe.

INGREDIENTS:

125 g mixed berries

45 g sugar

2 drops vanilla extract

70 g plain flour

2 tbsp rolled oats

40 g butter, melted

EQUIPMENT:

2 ramekins, 9 cm wide and 5 cm deep, or roughly 200 ml capacity

1   If using frozen berries, make sure they are fully thawed before you start. If using fresh berries, wash them thoroughly. Carefully cut away any leaves using a sharp knife and slice any large berries, such as strawberries, into smaller chunks about the size of a blueberry.

2   Preheat the air fryer to 200°C/400°F.

3   Divide the berries between the two ramekins so there are around the same amount in each.

4   Add 1 teaspoon of the sugar and a drop of vanilla extract to each of the ramekins. Give the berries a gentle stir to coat them in sugar and vanilla.

5   Use tongs to carefully put the ramekins into the basket of the air fryer. Set the timer to 5 minutes.

6   While the berries are cooking, add the flour and remaining sugar to a bowl, and stir.

7   Stir in the melted butter. This should make a crumbly mixture. Add the oats and stir them in, too.

8   When the berries are done, carefully remove the ramekins from the fryer using oven gloves, and place them on a plate or heatproof mat. The air fryer will be hot, so ask an adult for help here if you need it.

9   Sprinkle half of the crumble mixture on top of the berries in each ramekin. Carefully put the ramekins back into the air fryer using tongs or oven gloves. Set the timer to 6 minutes.

10   When the time is up, open the fryer. If the tops of the crumbles are golden and crunchy looking and you can see the berries underneath bubbling, carefully remove them from the fryer using tongs or oven gloves. If they don't look quite done, cook for a further 2–3 minutes before checking again.

11   Serve the crumbles warm with custard, cream or ice cream.

Apples work well with raisins and cinnamon, or rhubarb. With cooking apples or rhubarb, add an extra teaspoon of sugar to each ramekin to offset the tartness of the fruit.

CHEF IT UP!

Why not experiment with different fruits?

CHOCOLATE CHIP COOKIES

MAKES 12 COOKIES | TAKES 30-40 MINUTES

What makes these cookies the best? It's not because they are the perfect blend of crunchy, chewy and chocolatey (they are). It's because you can make a batch almost as quickly as you can eat it!

INGREDIENTS:

70 g brown sugar

100 g butter, melted

50 g caster sugar

½ tsp salt

½ tsp vanilla extract

200 g plain flour

1 medium egg, beaten

100 g chocolate chips

1. Add the melted butter, sugar, salt and vanilla to a large bowl and mix with a wooden spoon. Don't worry if the butter and sugar don't mix completely, this will be fixed in the next step.

2. Add the flour and the egg and mix until you have a thick, sticky dough. Add the chocolate chips and stir gently until the chips are distributed evenly throughout the mixture.

3. Place a liner paper into your air fryer basket. Scoop a heaped tablespoon of cookie dough from the bowl and scrape if off the spoon onto the piece of liner paper. Squash the blob of dough slightly with the back of a spoon. You don't need to flatten it completely as the cookies will spread while they bake.

4. Scoop another tablespoon of dough out of the bowl and scrape it onto the liner paper 4–5 cm from the first, and squash it with the back of your spoon. Repeat this until your liner paper is covered with blobs of dough. You will likely have to cook the cookies in batches.

5. Put the basket into the air fryer. Set the temperature to 160°C/320°F and the timer to 12 minutes.

6. When the time is up, open the fryer and look at your cookies. If they have spread out and look a little dry on top, use a spatula to carefully slide the cookies out of the fryer and onto a wire rack. If they still look quite doughy, put them back into the air fryer for 2 minutes, and then check again.

7. Leave the cookies for 10 minutes. They should firm up a bit as they cool.

8. Serve with an ice-cold glass of milk.

Experiment to find your perfect signature cookie. You could try dark or white chocolate chips, dried fruit or nuts. Sweets such as M&Ms and Smarties work well, too. For a Christmas cookie, swap half or all the chocolate chips for crushed candy canes. Delicious!

BAKE-ANYTIME BISCUITS

MAKES 16–20 BISCUITS | TAKES 1 HOUR 30 MINUTES TO MAKE THE DOUGH, PLUS 8 MINUTES TO BAKE

Ever feel like a homemade biscuit, but don't want to make a whole batch? This biscuit dough can be kept in the fridge for a week. Simply cut a couple of slices and air fry them whenever you need a warm biscuit treat.

INGREDIENTS:

100 g caster sugar

100 g butter, soft

225 g plain flour

1 egg, beaten

½ tsp vanilla extract

1 tsp lemon zest

EQUIPMENT:

Electric whisk

1   Add the butter and sugar to a large bowl and mix with an electric whisk until the mixture is combined and is a light-yellow colour. If you don't have an electric whisk, use a wooden spoon and press the mixture against the side of the bowl until it comes together and is completely combined.

2   Add the flour, vanilla extract and lemon zest, and mix. Add the egg and mix until the ingredients form a dough.

3   Bring the dough together with your hands. If the dough is sticky, cover your hands in a little flour. Shape the dough into a log shape approximately 6 cm wide. Wrap the log in cling film and put it in the fridge for one hour, or up to a week.

4   When you are ready to bake, preheat the air fryer to 200°C/400°F.

5   Remove the biscuit log from the fridge and unwrap one end. Use a sharp knife to cut 1 cm thick slices of dough from the log. Cut as many slices as biscuits you want to bake. Rewrap the remaining dough and return it to the fridge.

6   Carefully place a liner into the basket of your air fryer. Use tongs to carefully arrange the slices of biscuit dough onto the liner. Try to leave at least 3 cm around each biscuit. You many need to work in batches. Set the timer to 8 minutes.

7   When the time is up, open the fryer. The biscuits should have turned a deeper yellow colour and should look dry on top. They may be a little browner around the edges. If the biscuits look a little raw, close the fryer and cook for another 2–3 minutes before checking again.

8   Carefully remove the biscuits from the fryer using tongs or a spatula and place onto a wire rack to cool for at least 5 minutes before serving.

SYRUP SPONGE PUDDING

SERVES 1 | TAKES 20 MINUTES

Serve yourself a single portion of the ultimate comfort dessert. This pudding, like most puddings, is even better when served with custard or a scoop of vanilla ice cream.

INGREDIENTS:

4 tbsp plain flour

½ tsp baking powder

3 tbsp milk or yoghurt

14 g butter, softened, plus a little extra for greasing

½ tsp salt

A few drops vanilla extract

3 tbsp golden syrup

1 tbsp boiling water

EQUIPMENT:

1 ramekin, 9 cm wide and 5 cm deep, or roughly 200 ml capacity

1   Preheat the air fryer to 200°C/400°F.

2   Dip a piece of kitchen roll in butter and rub it thoroughly around the inside of the ramekin. This will help stop your pudding from sticking to the sides. Add 1 tablespoon of golden syrup to the bottom of the ramekin.

3   Add the flour, baking powder, milk or yoghurt, butter, salt, vanilla extract and the rest of the syrup to a bowl. Mix the ingredients together, using a fork, until you have a smooth batter.

4   Spoon the mixture into the ramekin, making sure to leave at least 1–2 cm between the mixture and the top of the ramekin. You may need to use a silicone spatula to get all of the mixture from the sides of the bowl, as it is very sticky. Smooth down the top of your pudding using the back of a spoon.

5   Carefully pour 1 tablespoon of boiling water on top of your pudding. Do not stir it in.

6   Carefully cover the ramekin tightly with a piece of tin foil and use tongs to carefully put it into the basket of the air fryer. Set the timer to 15 minutes.

7   When the time is up, remove the pudding from the fryer using tongs or oven gloves and put it on a heatproof mat or plate. The air fryer will be hot, so ask an adult for help here if you need it.

8   Remove the tin foil. The pudding should look pale, but spring back when pressed. To be certain it is cooked, insert a table knife into the centre of the pudding. The knife should come out clean with only a few crumbs attached. If the knife comes out with raw batter on it, replace the foil and put it back in the fryer. Cook for another 3–5 minutes.

9   When the pudding is out of the fryer, run a knife all the way around the inside of the ramekin. Turn the ramekin upside down and put it on a plate. Give the ramekin a shake. The pudding should slide out covered in syrup. If it is stubborn, run your knife around the inside, and then try again. It may take a couple of tries.

10   If it is really stuck, never fear, serve it in the pot. It will still be delicious.

CHEF IT UP!

Try replacing the golden syrup with your favorite jam, or even chocolate spread!

INDEX